Andy Griffiths has been writing and creating stories in one form or another from the time he was old enough to pick up a pencil. He is the author of over 25 books, including nonsense verse, short stories, comic novels and plays—most of them illustrated by Terry Denton. Over the past 15 years Andy's books have been *New York Times* bestsellers, won over 50 children's choice awards and been adapted as a television cartoon series called *What's with Andy?* He is an ambassador for the Indigenous Literacy Foundation and The Pyjama Foundation. You can find out more information at www.andygriffiths.com.au

Terry Denton has been writing and illustrating children's books for 30 years. He is best known for his Gasp! books and TV series, the Wombat and Fox stories and his 20 books in collaboration with Andy Griffiths. He won the Australian CBC Picture Book of the Year Award in 1986 and has since been short-listed for many awards both in Australia and internationally. His work has won more than 40 children's choice awards throughout Australia.
You can find out more information at www.terry.denton.com

Once upon a SLIME

ANDY GRIFFITHS
illustrated by TERRY DENTON

Pan
Pan Macmillan Australia

First published 2013 in Pan by Macmillan Australia Pty Limited
1 Market Street, Sydney

National Library of Australia
Cataloguing-in-Publication data:

Griffiths, Andy

Once upon a slime : 45 ways
to get writing–fast! / Andy
Griffiths; Terry Denton, illustrator.

9781742612096 (pbk.)
Composition (Language arts)
Storytelling–Study and teaching (Primary)

Denton, Terry, 1950-

372.623

Typeset in 12/16 Minion Pro by Liz Seymour, Seymour Designs
Photographs by James Penlidis (pp: 6, 95, 113, 149, 161, 313–317)
Printed by McPherson's Printing Group
The characters and events in this book are fictitious and any resemblance
to real persons, living or dead, is purely coincidental.

Papers used by Pan Macmillan Australia Pty Ltd are natural,
recyclable products made from wood grown in sustainable forests.
The manufacturing processes conform to the environmental
regulations of the country of origin.

Contents

Introduction

I wrote my first 'book' when I was eight years old—a get-well card for my dad. It was a piece of paper folded into three and was called *A Little Boooke I Madee*. It said, 'I hear your sick. So turn over the pages and see what you are if you don't get better.'

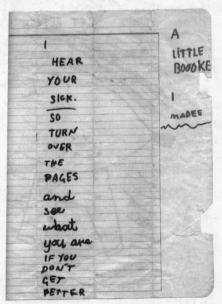

My first 'book'—and my first recorded spelling mistakes.

Then, when my poor sick father turned the pages he was greeted with this disturbing picture of himself as some sort of animal buried in the ground next to a tombstone that says DOOMED. (I'm not sure why I chose to draw him like this—maybe we had recently buried a dead pet in the backyard and I was worried we would have to do the same to him if he didn't get better!)

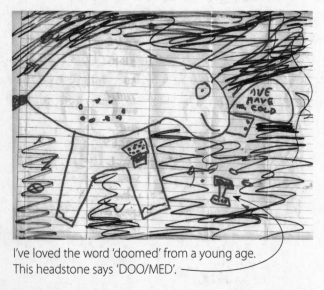

I've loved the word 'doomed' from a young age. This headstone says 'DOO/MED'.

So, basically, what I was telling him was: 'Get better soon … or you are DOOMED!' It might have been quite an unconventional approach for a get-well card, but it was effective because he got better really fast. I wasn't about to let it rest at that, however.

As the years went on I dedicated myself to making the most terrifying get-well cards ever invented, as this one I made when I was ten clearly shows:

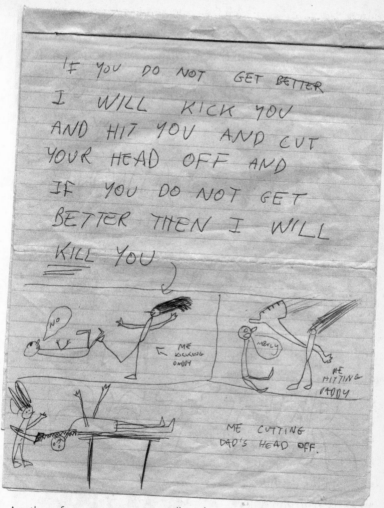

Another of my gruesome get-well cards.

Anyway, I think you get the general idea. All I can say is it was pretty fortunate that I grew up to be a writer and not a doctor.

When I wasn't making gruesome cards, another thing I liked to do was fill my NOTHING TO DO BOOK with lots of stuff that I was interested in, like newspaper photos, advertisements for horror movies and bubblegum cards.

Without knowing it, I was creating a writing journal … but I didn't think of it as that—I just thought of it as a way of having fun.

My childhood diary.

One of the things I liked doing in my book was cutting out photographs from the newspaper and messing around with them. 'I've got a splitting headache' was an early triumph. Okay, okay, I admit it's not *that* funny … but check out the crazy photo on the next page.

An early attempt at humour.

4

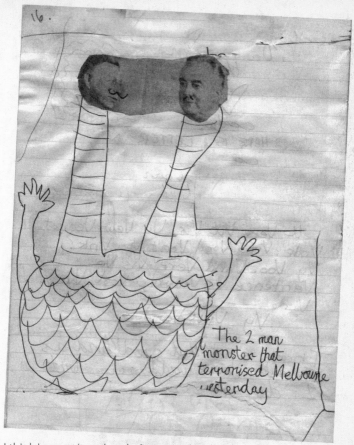

I think I meant 'two-headed monster'.

Yeah, I know, I know ... it's not that funny either—and my cartoons weren't much better—but the important thing is I was having fun, and that's pretty much the theme of this book.

You don't have to be a great artist—or a great speller—to be able to have a great time with words and pictures.

No prizes for the correct answer.

One day I was hanging around the second-hand stall at our school fete and I was lucky enough to pick up this rusty old typewriter for 40 cents. I carried it home, my dad got it working and then I borrowed a typing book and taught myself to touch type.

I still have the old typewriter I bought at my primary school fete.

I spent many hours practising by typing out passages from my favourite books. (I didn't know it at the time, but this is actually a great way for a beginning writer to find out how stories work!) It wasn't long before I was using my rapidly developing typing skills to produce a magazine full of jokes and funny news articles for the other students in my year 7 class.

I used to sell my magazine 'Popcorn' for 3 cents a copy.

I was thirteen years old when I had my first short story published in *Pursuit* magazine. It was called 'Lost in time' and was about going to a cricket match at the MCG and being mysteriously transported many centuries into the future.

That's me!

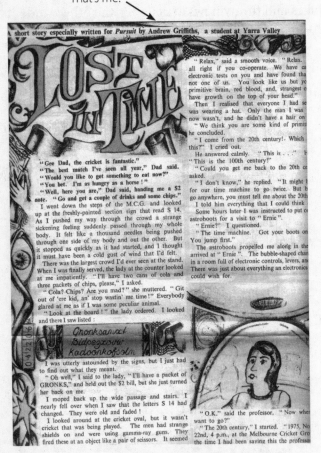

My first-ever published short story. (You can read the exciting conclusion at www.andygriffiths.com.au/about)

I spent the rest of my teenage years writing stories, poems, songs and cartoons for the amusement of myself and my friends and when, in my late 20s, I became a secondary English teacher I began writing stories to amuse my students. I published a number of these as 12-page pocket books, which I sold at markets.

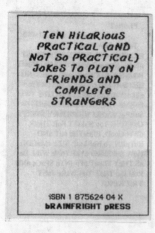

The first version of *Just Tricking!* was a 12-page pocket book.

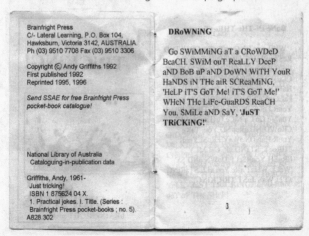

Brainfright Press
C/- Lateral Learning, P.O. Box 104,
Hawksburn, Victoria 3142, AUSTRALIA.
Ph (03) 9510 7708 Fax (03) 9510 3306

Copyright © Andy Griffiths 1992
First published 1992
Reprinted 1995, 1996

*Send SSAE for free Brainfright Press
pocket-book catalogue!*

National Library of Australia
Cataloguing-in-publication data

Griffiths, Andy, 1961-
  Just tricking!
  ISBN 1 875624 04 X.
  1. Practical jokes. I. Title. (Series :
  Brainfright Press pocket-books ; no. 5).
A828.302

DRoWNiNG

Go SWiMMiNG aT a CRoWDeD BeaCH. SWiM ouT ReaLLY DeeP aND BoB uP aND DoWN WiTH YouR HaNDS iN THe aiR SCReaMiNG, 'HeLP iT'S GoT Me! iT'S GoT Me!' WHeN THe LiFe-GuaRDS ReaCH You, SMiLe aND SaY, '**JuST TRiCKiNG!**'

3

9

Many of the short pieces I wrote during this period were published in 1993 as a creative-writing textbook called *Swinging on the Clothesline*. This book was notable for being both my first published book and for introducing me to Terry Denton, who was commissioned by the publisher to illustrate it.

I loved Terry's illustrating style and we worked together on another collection of creative-writing ideas called *Rubbish Bins in Space* in 1995.

These books are now out of print and no longer available, but *Once upon a Slime* is basically a rewritten and revised version of them, using examples from all the books I have written since 1997.

My first two books ever published were creative-writing textbooks.

Two years later, the first Just book, *Just Tricking!*, was published. This book was notable for being both my first published book of pure short stories and for introducing me to the editor, Jill, who is now my wife and who has edited every book since then. She is also the inspiration for the character Jill in the Treehouse series.

Jill (in her flying-cat sleigh) arriving at Andy and Terry's treehouse (*The 13-Storey Treehouse*).

only available as an ebook

So, as you can see, I have enjoyed having fun with words and pictures in some way or another from an early age, and still do. In this book I will show you 45 ways you can too.

1. Bad Mummy
& Daddy cartoons

Some of my favourite characters in all of the books that
Terry and I have created are Bad Mummy, Bad Daddy and
the kid who always asks permission to do something really
stupid and/or dangerous. Most normal parents would say
no, but I wanted to play with the idea of parents who do
the opposite, that is, say yes when they should say no. They
then surprise us again when, instead of being upset at what
happens to their child as a result of their bad parenting,
they simply shrug and say, 'Oops!'

Bad Mummy and the very busy six-lane highway

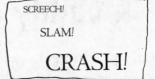

THE END

The Bad Book

See if you can match the first frames of these Bad Mummy and Bad Daddy cartoons with the last frames on the next page.

I love creating characters who do or say the opposite to what you would expect and there are many examples of these in my books and stories—especially the Bad Book series. These include the bad dentist, the bad vet, the three bad guys and the bad teacher (pictured below).

Note: Vegetables are NOT bad for you.

The Bad Teacher (*The Very Bad Book*)

TRY THIS

Draw your own Bad Mummy cartoon

Draw up nine boxes on a page. Think of the most dangerous, silly, crazy thing that a child could possibly want to do. Have them ask their parent for permission to do this crazy thing in the first frame. Then, after some discussion of the possible dangers of the activity, have the parent give in and say yes. Then show us what happens next. Don't forget to have the parent say, 'Oops!' at the end.

Feel free to borrow any of the following titles to get you started:

- Bad Mummy and the electric fence
- Bad Mummy and the chainsaw-wielding zombie
- Bad Mummy and the killer whale
- Bad Mummy and the poisonous poison
- Bad Mummy and the cute fluffy bunny rabbit
- Bad Mummy and the whirlpool
- Bad Mummy and the stick of dynamite
- Bad Mummy and the crocodile-infested river
- Bad Mummy and the very sharp knives

PLAYING WITH KNIVES CAN BE DANGEROUS.

2. Characters

When I started out writing the stories that would eventually become the book *Just Tricking!*, I tried to write stories with completely made-up characters. But the characters didn't feel 'real' to me. After a while I found it worked much better if I pretended I was writing true stories about me and my friends at school.

I 'borrowed' and exaggerated certain aspects of my best friend, Danny Pickett, as well as the feelings I had for the girl I secretly admired, Lisa Mackney. I even cast myself (or a version of myself) as the narrator.

Danny Pickett   Lisa Mackney   Me

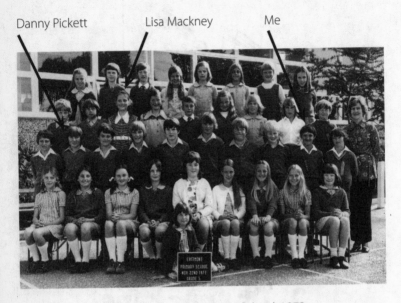

Grade 5, Eastmont Primary School, 1972

Here's a photo of us all in grade 5 with our teacher, Mrs Jensen. On my school report she commented that I had a good sense of humour. I think whoever gave me that haircut had one too. (Thanks, Dad!)

In real life Danny Pickett was—and still is—a very funny and fun-loving person. Sure, he did the occasional dumb thing, but he is not the idiot Andy makes him out to be, and in real life I am not quite as foolhardy and impulsive and selfish as Andy the character. Part of the fun of storytelling is that you can change whatever you like to make the stories more entertaining.

Highly exaggerated version of Danny and Andy.

Andy and Lisa as Macbeth and Lady Macbeth.

I also based other characters in the Just series on my parents, my neighbours and even my dog, Sooty. In real life I have two younger sisters called Susan and Julie, but I combined them into one sister, Jen (named after my friend Mark's sister), and made her older than Andy because I thought it would be easier for him to embarrass and annoy an older sister (especially in front of her boyfriend).

Likewise, I based the characters in the Treehouse series on Terry Denton (the illustrator), myself (the writer) and my wife Jill (who is an editor). In real life the three of us work on the books together, having fun, dreaming up silly stuff and solving problems. Once again, however, I must point out that Terry is not as irresponsible or as annoying in real life, I'm not quite as bossy and Jill doesn't have loads of animals, though she did used to have a cat called Silky.

Andy and Terry working together in *The 26-Storey Treehouse*.

In *The 26-Storey Treehouse* Jill helps Andy and Terry cure the sharks when they get sick after eating Terry's dirty underpants.

Sometimes I base my characters on types of people rather than specific people. In the Schooling Around series many of the characters are named according to their dominant personality traits.

Characters from the Schooling Around series.

For example, Mrs Cross is always cross, Mr Shush the librarian is always telling the students to shush, Fiona McBrain is really smart, Grant Gadget is always inventing crazy machines and devices, Gretel Armstrong is very strong and Mr Grunt is a vain, boastful sports teacher.

I also like naming characters after their physical characteristics. For example, Mr Big Nose has a very big nose, Captain Woodenhead the pirate has a head made of wood and Lumpyhead Fred has a very lumpy head.

Mr Big Nose from the Treehouse books.

Lumpy-head Fred from *The Big Fat Cow That Goes Kapow*.

Captain Woodenhead from *The 26-Storey Treehouse*.

Common to all of these methods of coming up with characters, though, is that they all involve a certain degree of exaggeration. I tend to select one quality of a person and then exaggerate it. If a character is bad, I make them REALLY bad. If they're boring, I make them REALLY boring. The more exaggerated, the more comic a character tends to become.

A fast way of establishing a character's personality is to simply let them speak for themselves.

See if you can match the following quotes to the character descriptions on page 26.

1 Second place is just another word for first loser.

2 bark bark bark bark bark bark bark bark

3 Mum! John said that I look like I came out of a dog's bottom!

4 It's rare to see such thoughtfulness in young people today. They're all too wrapped up in their Xboxes and mobile phones and eePods.

5 If God had meant us to *catch* bums, she wouldn't have given us bumblasters to blast them with!

6 It wasn't until he had the scimitar at my throat that I was able to reach deep within myself and produce the burp that saved my life!

A. Mr Bainbridge, a self-important man who doesn't necessarily know what he's talking about but always has an opinion.

B. Mr Grunt, a boastful, insulting sports teacher who is obsessed with winning.

C. Betty, a long-suffering piece of dog poo who is always being teased by her brother.

D. Barky the Barking Dog, a stupid dog that never stops barking.

E. Eleanor Sterne, a ferocious, violent, hot-tempered bum-fighter.

F. Ms Livingstone, resourceful, courageous, intrepid stuntwoman/ adventurer/schoolteacher.

Answers: 1B, 2D, 3C, 4A, 5E, 6F

TRY THIS

Guess who?

The aim of this exercise is to describe a person in such a way that somebody else who also knows that person would be able to guess who it is. Don't reveal the person's name or relationship to you. You can describe what they look like but also let us hear them speaking. What sort of things do they typically say and how do they say them? Let us see them in action. What sort of things do they typically do and how do they do them? Let us see their possessions. What sort of things do they typically have in their hands and how do they use them?

Be alert for any detail—no matter how small—that will help you to convey in as few words as possible who that person is. Use the following list to help you choose somebody to describe:

- Parent
- Grandparent
- Sister/Brother
- Cousin
- Friend
- Neighbour
- Teacher
- Yourself

Read your description aloud to a friend, family member or your class and see if they can guess who it is. Have fun, but don't write anything that might upset the person you're describing if they were to hear it.

... OR THIS

Write a story starring YOU!

You don't have to be able to make up imaginary characters or exotic settings to tell a good story. A fast way to create fun, believable-sounding stories is to start with the character you know best in the whole world (YOU!). Choose one of the following scenarios and describe what you would do and what happens next.

- You wake up to discover that you can no longer speak—you can only bark like a dog.

- You are in class. It's a hot day. Your friend starts taking off their clothes ... their shirt ... their shoes ... their socks ... their *pants*!

- You have a strong suspicion that your teacher is a vampire and, worse still, you suspect that they know you have discovered their secret.

Note: See Chapter 37 Snapshots (page 266) if you're not sure how to get started. See Chapter 45 What if ...? (page 329) and Chapter 43 Toy stories (page 313) if you'd like to keep your story going. And see Chapter 41 The day my BLANK went BLANK! (page 299) to help you come up with an attention-grabbing title.

3. Choose your own adventure

One of the things I really like about the early stages of writing a story is wondering about all the possible things that could happen. But one of the things I really *don't* like about writing is having to make a decision about which one of those things to choose. That's why I love writing in the 'Choose your own adventure' format—because you can dream up lots of possibilities and have fun exploring them all.

'Cake of Doom' in *Just Disgusting!* was the first choose-your-own story I wrote. The challenge is you have to bake a cake for your mother without getting killed in one of 11 (admittedly highly unlikely) cake-baking accidents.

CaKE OF DOOM:
a choose your own baking adventure

Baking a cake: a recipe for success or a recipe for disaster? It's up to you: in this story the decisions are yours.

Your name is Andy. Tomorrow is Mother's Day and you've decided to surprise your mother by getting up early and baking her a cake. The only problem is that you've never baked a cake before but, hey, you're not going to let a minor detail like that stop you.

Good luck, happy baking, and whatever you do, BE CAREFUL!

Writing this story as a 'Choose your own adventure' allowed me to explore the many possible (as well as highly improbable) accidents you could have while trying to bake a cake.

See if you can match the cause of each of the following cake-baking accidents with the fatal results on page 32.

Cake-baking accidents

1
You reach up to get the packet-cake mix from a high shelf in the cupboard and accidentally dislodge a bowling ball that was hidden there.

2
You put the cake into the oven, turn the gas on but forget to light it.

3
You make icing for the cake but accidentally use rat poison instead of icing sugar.

4
You forget to put the lid on the blender before you switch it on and it splatters all over the kitchen like an erupting volcano.

5
You use your mother's new super-powerful food blender to grate a carrot and end up grating your fingers as well.

6
You accidentally put your dog into the oven and his tail catches on fire.

Fatal results

A

You run from the kitchen to get away from the mess and a little old lady in a wheelchair knocks you down and runs over your head. You die.

B

A bowling ball falls down and hits you on the head. You die.

C

You try to extinguish your dog's burning tail in the toilet but you accidentally flush your dog away. Your dog-loving mother finds out. You die.

D

Your whole family dies of rat poisoning. You are sentenced to death for their murders. You die.

E

All the blood leaks out of your body from your freshly grated finger stubs. You die.

F

You light a match and the whole kitchen explodes. You explode. You die.

Answers: 1B, 2F, 3D, 4A, 5E, 6C

TRY THIS

What happens next?

Choose one of the following scenarios (or invent one of your own) and come up with six different possibilities for what might happen next—the more entertaining and outlandish the better.

1. You're cooking pancakes. You flip one and it flies out of the window ... (Where does the pancake go? What trouble might it cause?)

2. You're out riding your bike. You hit a banana skin and skid out of control ...

3. You are babysitting your very naughty five-year-old cousin. It's going pretty well until you turn around and see ...

4. You're just going to sleep and you notice a spider walking across the ceiling towards you ...

Note: The main point of the exercise is to practise generating lots of options for your stories. But if you're really inspired, why not use your favourite scenario—and imagined possibilities—as the starting point for a longer story (either choose-your-own style or traditional).

... OR THIS

Twelve doors

Imagine that you are standing in front of twelve doors. Behind one there is a fabulous treasure. Behind the others are eleven of the most dangerous things in the world. Draw or describe what lies behind each one.

4. Crazy machines and inventions

When I was young I used to read comics and they always had great ads for magic tricks and gadgets on the back pages, things like X-ray glasses, secret agent spy cameras and joy-buzzers. I was always intrigued by these and I guess that's why I enjoy dreaming up weird and wonderful gadgets and inventions for Terry to draw ... as you can see from the following examples.

HE INTRODUCED ME TO HIS GANG OF CRIMINAL MASTERMIND PALS, WHO WERE PUTTING THE FINISHING TOUCHES TO AN EVIL UNDERPANTS-SHRINKING MACHINE.

THEY PLANNED TO USE IT TO SHRINK THE UNDERPANTS OF ALL THE POLICE IN THE ENTIRE WORLD AT THE EXACT SAME TIME!

Underpants shrinker/expander
('A really, really good excuse', *Just Shocking!*)

'No problem,' says Terry. 'I'll use my new super-flexible, endlessly extendable, titanium-coated talking tube instead.'

Terry's super-flexible, endlessly extendable, titanium-coated talking tube (*The 26-Storey Treehouse*)

Direct-to-brain information delivery helmet *(The 13-Storey Treehouse)*

Banana enlarger *(The 13-Storey Treehouse)*

Mashing and pulverising machine *(Just Macbeth!)*

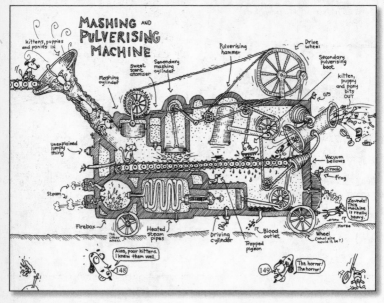

Underpants-washing machine
(The 26-Storey Treehouse)

'Well,' he says, 'I came up with the idea of using the shark tank to wash my underpants. I dangled a dummy over the top of the water and the sharks thought it was a real person, and were jumping all around trying to bite it, and that churned up the water—you know, like in a washing machine.

Vegetable vaporiser
(The 13-Storey Treehouse)

Eventually I found him down in the secret underground laboratory.

Water-measuring machine
(The 13-Storey Treehouse)

Experimental, armoured, bicycle-powered miniature submarine
(The 26-Storey Treehouse)

Automatic tattoo machine
(The 26-Storey Treehouse)

TRY THIS

Design your own crazy machine

Include labels explaining how your machine
works and what it does. If you need help coming
up with an idea, why not design one of the
following machines?

- A homework machine
- A brother-disappearing machine
- A spider-killing machine
- A machine to help a horse travel through
  a canary
- A machine to turn a cat into a dog
- A machine to make time go backwards ...
  or faster ... or slower ... or stop completely
- A machine that will make exact copies of
  anything you put into it: objects, money,
  food ... even you!
- A machine that will make you invisible
- A machine that can travel on the ground,
  through water and through the air
- A machine to erase your parents' memories
- A machine to make someone fall in love
  with you
- A machine for controlling the weather
- A machine to stop the dog next door barking
- A machine for making small things large
- A machine for making large things small

5. Danger! Danger!

Many of my stories feature characters in very dangerous situations or doing very dangerous things. Often they find themselves doing very dangerous things in very dangerous situations, like the little boy trapped in the burning apartment in *The 26-Storey Treehouse*.

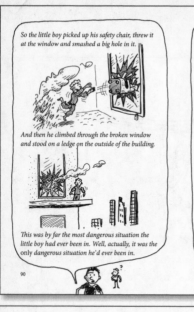

So the little boy picked up his safety chair, threw it at the window and smashed a big hole in it.

And then he climbed through the broken window and stood on a ledge on the outside of the building.

This was by far the most dangerous situation the little boy had ever been in. Well, actually, it was the only dangerous situation he'd ever been in.

90

He looked down at the ground below—a long, long, long way below.

He looked back into his bedroom, which was now completely on fire.

He knew jumping from the top floor of a very tall apartment tower was an extremely dangerous thing to do, but he knew that staying in a burning apartment was extremely dangerous too. Possibly even more extremely dangerous than jumping from the top floor of a very tall apartment tower.

91

So he jumped.

92

93

The 26-Storey Treehouse

Sometimes imaginary danger can be just as scary as actual danger. In this passage from *Treasure Fever!*, Jack Japes imagines a reason why their teacher is running late.

'What if she's been in an accident?' said Newton.

'I don't think that's likely,' said Jenny. 'You know how careful Mrs Chalkboard is.'

'Yes, but careful people can still be involved in accidents,' said Fiona. 'That's why they are called *accidents*. Something may have happened to the bus.'

Newton's face was getting whiter and whiter, if that was even possible.

'Yeah,' said Jack, taking up where Fiona left off. 'There might have been an oil spill on the road and the bus skidded and went over a cliff … into shark-infested water … and the sharks got into the bus and all the passengers got eaten alive … and all that was left was their skeletons. Then imagine if Mrs Chalkboard's skeleton climbed back up the cliff and hitched a ride to school and then came in the classroom and—'

'JACK!' said Jenny, 'for goodness' sake, STOP IT! You're scaring Newton to death! I'm sure Mrs Chalkboard is fine!'

Jack Japes terrorises poor Newton Hooton with his worst case scenario about why their teacher is late (*Treasure Fever!*).

Of course, no road in real life could be as dangerous as The Very Bad Road in *The Very Bad Book* ...

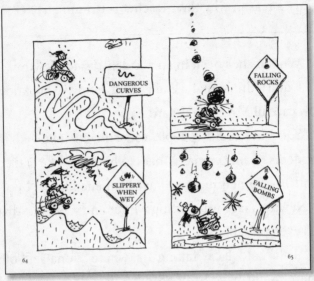

The Very Bad Book

In the Just series, Andy constantly finds himself in extremely dangerous situations. Some of these include:

- Riding in a pram down a steep hill ('Runaway pram', *Just Stupid!*)
- Flying high above the ground attached to helium balloons ('A crazy ... idea', *Just Crazy!*)
- Being buried alive ('Playing dead', *Just Tricking!*)
- Jumping from a motorbike onto a moving car ('Are we there yet?', *Just Annoying!*)

- Helping to steer a car while Danny is asleep at the wheel ('Sleepover of doom', *Just Doomed!*)

- Being chased around the bath by two mysterious brown blobs ('Two brown blobs', *Just Disgusting!*)

- Being trapped in a shower that is filling up with water ('In the shower with Andy', *Just Annoying!*)

- Flying off a clothesline at high speed ('Swinging on the clothesline', *Just Annoying!*)

- Being chased by angry nude people ('Just nude!', *Just Doomed!*)

It seems like the more dangerous the situation, the more readers love it. I guess stories allow us to have the thrill of experiencing dangerous situations without the risk of actual injury.

TRY THIS

Bad Road cartoon

Draw your own bad road cartoon.

Try to think of all the things you are most scared of and see if you can include these as hazards along the way.

The structure of these cartoons is very simple—one road sign and one bad thing happening per frame. If you need ideas, feel free to help yourself to some from the list below.

- Falling rocks, falling zombies, falling elephants, exploding elephants
- Slippery when wet, explosive when wet
- Naked people ahead
- Micro sleeps can kill, micro sheep can kill
- Beware invisible cows

... OR THIS

Why Mrs Chalkboard is late

Write a letter of apology from Mrs Chalkboard—or, even better, your own teacher—to the principal explaining why you were late for class. You can use the scenario from the *Treasure Fever!* extract or you can come up with your own exciting, ridiculously dangerous reasons.

6. Diary of a blank

Day-by-day accounts of what happens to you—or a fictional character—are an interesting alternative to a traditional narrative. A diary can be based on true events, exaggerated events, completely made-up events or a combination of all three, like 'The very bad holiday' on the following page. I'll let you decide what might have been true, what's exaggerated and what is completely made up.

The Very Bad Holiday

The Very Bad Book

Just Shocking! features a series of 'Truly shocking days' diary entries.

Diaries don't only have to be told from the point of view of a human being. They can be told from the point of view of almost anything: fridges, horses, knives, garden gnomes ... even bums. They all have a story to tell.

What sort of jokes would a horse like? *(Just Macbeth!)*

What dreams
might a knife have?
(Just Macbeth!)

Should we trust our fridges?
(Just Crazy!)

In 'Romeo and Juliet and Danny and Lisa and me: a diary of doomed love', Andy tells the story of a school production of *Romeo and Juliet* in a series of diary entries.

WEEK 1

Monday November 8th

I just landed the part of Romeo in the school production of *Romeo and Juliet*. To tell you the truth, I see myself as more of a Hollywood action hero than a Shakespearean actor, but I tried out for the part of Romeo because I knew that Lisa Mackney had already been chosen for the role of Juliet and I figured it was probably the best chance I'm ever going to get to kiss her.

From 'Romeo and Juliet' (*Just Doomed!*)

I chose to tell the story in the format of a series of diary entries as it allowed me to quickly dip in and out of crucial and dramatic moments during the three-week rehearsal period covered by the story. As the night of the performance draws closer, it helps to create a sense of urgency.

(Needless to say, Andy's scheme does not go according to plan and he doesn't get to kiss Lisa!)

TRY THIS

Truly shocking days diary

Create a diary entry—or series of entries—based on exaggerating (either slightly or majorly) the small problems you encounter in everyday life. The smaller the problem, the funnier it is when you exaggerate it.

- Burnt the toast
- Can't find matching socks
- Only one flake left in the cornflakes packet
- Shoelace keeps coming undone
- Thought it was Saturday but it was Friday
- Wore book character dress-up on the wrong day

... OR THIS

Diary of a blank (you fill in the blank)

Imagine life from the point of view of your pet, your underpants, or one of your most treasured possessions (assuming that your underpants are not one of your most treasured possessions). Write a diary of a typical week in their life. What would be the highlights and/or lowlights?

7. DO's & DON'Ts

As you can see from this photo, I was a keen reader from an early age. (Also a very snappy dresser!)

The first book I ever loved was an old German book that my grandma owned called *Der Struwwelpeter* (1845), which translates as *Shock-headed Peter*.

DO sit quietly and read a book.

The stories were cautionary tales about children who behaved badly. For example, Shock-headed Peter was a dirty boy who never washed or cut his hair and nails. (Note the subtitle: Merry Stories & Funny Pictures!)

Struwwelpeter

Merry Stories & Funny Pictures

DO cut your hair and fingernails.

DON'T suck your thumb … or else!

Other bad children in the book included Harriet, who played with matches, and Little Suck-a-thumb, who would not stop sucking his thumb. Of course, these children suffered horribly for their crimes. Harriet was reduced to a little pile of ashes and the unfortunate Little Suck-a-thumb had his thumbs cut off by a long-legged man with a big pair of scissors (just as his mother had warned him he would!).

I found the book scary … but kind of funny, too. I don't think reading it scared me into behaving properly, but it did teach me something very important—that reading could be really exciting, surprising and lots of fun.

And, of course, it inspired me to write my own cautionary tales. Some of these are 'The girl who asked too many questions', 'The boy who ate dead flies' and 'The boy who forgot his head because it wasn't screwed on'.

Unfortunately, cautionary tales rarely have happy endings. The boy who forgot his head ends up spending the rest of his life headless … and pantsless.

(Moral: If you're going to unscrew your head, don't forget to screw it back on again.)

DON'T forget to screw your head on … or put on your pants (*The Very Bad Book*).

The boy who ate dead flies grows wings and flies around the room and into the kitchen, where his mother mistakes him for a fly and swats him. (Moral: Don't eat dead flies.)

DON'T eat dead flies
(*The Very Bad Book*).

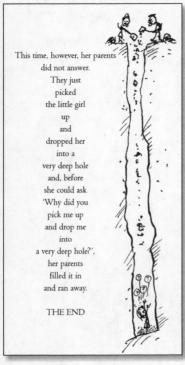

The Bad Book

And the girl who asked too many questions ends up being buried in a very deep hole by her exhausted parents. (Moral: DON'T annoy your parents by asking too many questions, especially if they are the type of people who are likely to bury you in a hole in the ground if you ask too many questions.)

One of my favourite cautionary tales in *The Very Bad Book* is the one about the three bad guys who come up with the very bad idea of not washing their hands after going to the toilet, picking their noses and touching pets and other animals.

The three bad guys from *The Very Bad Book*.

Predictably, as in all good cautionary tales, their bad behaviour results in them all suffering a variety of very serious illnesses, including supercalifragilisticexpialidosis.

The three bad guys come to a bad end (*The Very Bad Book*).

Of course, not all cautionary tales need to be presented as stories. They can simply be an illustrated list of DOs and DON'Ts, like this guide to table manners.

TABLE MANNERS: DO's and DON'Ts

DO use a knife and fork

DON'T eat like a dog

DO be polite and considerate to other diners

DON'T start food fights

DO eat until you feel you've had an elegant sufficiency

DON'T eat till you burst

DO ask permission to leave the table when finished

DON'T jump up, yell 'I win!', tip the table over and run away

TRY THIS

Illustrate a list of DO's and DON'Ts

Write and illustrate a list of six DO's and six DON'Ts for one or more of the following situations:

- In the classroom
- At the football
- At Grandma's house
- At the dinner table
- In a fancy restaurant
- On a sleepover
- In the forest when you meet a big bad wolf

... OR THIS

Write a cautionary tale

Choose a title from the list below if you'd like some help getting started.

- The girl who never said please or thank you
- The boy who picked his nose
- The dog who chased cars
- The boy who rode his pet rabbit

SOME DINING TIPS:

Firstly, attract the waiter's attention.

Always explore the delights of exotic cuisine.

WHEN YOUR MEAL ARRIVES:

Remember good table manners,

and always spit out the plate.

IM
JUST
STUPID.

8. Dumb things

We've all had dumb ideas and done dumb things. The trouble with dumb ideas is that they often seem like brilliant ideas until you actually do them. My character Andy in the Just series knows this better than anybody. He has had a lot of dumb ideas and done a lot of dumb things. (And yes, most of his dumb ideas have come from dumb ideas that I have actually had!)

BEFORE

AFTER

'Hey, I know … I'll seal the shower up with silicone … then it will fill up with water!'

BEFORE

AFTER

'Hey, I know … it will be fun to get Danny to push me around in a pram!'

BEFORE

AFTER

'Hey, I know how to get this cockroach out of my pants—I'll just take them off, hang them out the bathroom window and shake them!'

BEFORE

AFTER

'Hey, I know how to make Jeremy Smart look bad in front of the whole school. I'll dive into the pool and save the drowning boy and then say that Jeremy pushed the poor kid in in the first place.'

BEFORE

AFTER

'Hey, I know how to get my rubber duck out of the rubbish bin … I'll just lean down into the bin and grab it!'

BEFORE

AFTER

'Hey, I know … I'll attach myself to this big bunch of weather balloons and Danny will hold the rope and I can go for a short, controlled float.'

But if you think Andy is dumb, look at Terry's track record.
He makes Andy look like a genius.

The 26-Storey Treehouse

TRY THIS

'Dumb things I've done' illustrated list

Write and illustrate a list of five dumb things you've done. These could be big things, small things, things from your past or things you did recently. If you are really smart and have never done—or thought of doing—anything dumb, then make a list of dumb things other people have done.

... OR THIS

Hey, I know ... Before & After pic

BEFORE

AFTER

Hey, I know ...

Draw a BEFORE picture of yourself having a dumb idea. Write a sentence under your picture explaining what your idea is. Then draw an AFTER picture showing the result of your dumb idea. Put all your pictures together to make a class book called *Dumb Things Our Class Has Done*. Put it in your library and share your dumbness with the rest of the school.

9. Everyday epics

Have you ever heard the expression 'making mountains out of molehills'? It means to treat a small problem as if it were a really big one. This is something comic characters do a lot. In fact, it's one of the things that makes them comic characters.

In 'Two brown blobs' Andy manages to turn a common bathtime mishap into a nightmarish struggle for survival.

'Two brown blobs' (*Just Disgusting!*)

There are many other examples of Just stories in which Andy makes a big deal out of a small thing or turns a simple procedure into a lengthy drama. I think of these as everyday epics. They include:

- 'Busting'
  Andy's desperate attempt to find a toilet in a multi-level shopping centre becomes an epic journey, during the course of which he accidentally causes the shopping centre to catch fire ... Luckily he has exactly what the firefighters need to extinguish the blaze.

Just Stupid!

REMOVING A BANDAID BY PIANO.

- 'Band-aid'
  Andy manages to make the removal of a band-aid a drama of Shakespearean proportions. ('To peel or not to peel? That is the question.')

  Just Stupid!

- 'Lick'
  Andy is trying to have the first lick of his ice-cream, but is constantly interrupted by friends, family and seagulls.

Just Doomed!

- 'The last Jaffa'
  Andy is at the cinema watching a James Bond movie when he drops the last lolly in his packet. Inspired by the movie, he decides to go on a Bond-style mission to find his last Jaffa, much to the annoyance of the other cinema patrons.

Just Annoying!

- 'Rubbish'
  Andy tries to put the rubbish bin out for collection but ends up falling into the bin, being tipped into the truck and going on a very disgusting journey.

Just Crazy!

- 'Mudmen'

Andy and his dad make their way through the neighbourhood naked and covered in mud on a quest to retrieve a set of house keys from Dad's office. Their adventure ends up being a transformative journey of personal discovery for Andy's father.

CRAZY FOR LIFE.

CHIRP

What is Dad on about? Obviously the stress of being locked out of his house without any clothes on has driven him over the edge.

'Dad,' I say, 'do you know what you're saying? Are you crazy?'

'Yes,' says Dad, putting his arm around my shoulders. 'I'm crazy all right. Crazy for life! I want to take more chances, climb more mountains, swim more rivers and watch more sunsets. Life's too short to waste, Andy. You, me, Mum and Jen—we're going to escape this ratrace. We're going to leave the city. We're going to live off the land—in the wild—in the raw.'

I'm a little worried about how our new life is going to work exactly, and what Mum and Jen are going to think about it when they get back home, but speaking for myself, I think it sounds kind of fun.

Crazy, but fun.

Just Crazy!

TRY THIS

Luckily / Unluckily story

Write a Luckily/Unluckily sequence based on a simple problem, either from your own life or from the list on page 76.

Even the most 'ordinary' life is full of the types of problems and challenges that can be used as the basis for fun stories. For example:

Luckily it was a curriculum day and I didn't have to go to school.

 Unluckily I had to go to the dentist.

Luckily it was only a check-up.

 Unluckily the dentist found a big hole in my tooth.

Luckily there was only one hole.

 Unluckily it was such a BIG hole that the dentist didn't have enough tooth-filling material to fill it.

Luckily some workers were fixing the footpath outside and the dentist was able to borrow some concrete.

 Unluckily the dentist used too much and concreted my mouth shut.

Luckily I'm quite good at drinking through my nose.

Luckily / Unluckily story starters:

1.
Luckily I got a kite for my birthday.
Unluckily it got stuck in a tree.
Luckily ...

2.
Luckily I was the first one up so I didn't have to wait to use the shower.
Unluckily I was getting out of the shower when I realised there were no towels in the bathroom.
Luckily ...

3.
Luckily I got a new bike.
Unluckily while I was riding it through the park a dog started chasing me.
Luckily ...

4.
Luckily my basketball team made it into the grand final.
Unluckily some idiot threw a banana peel onto the court.
Luckily ...

Please excuse
the empty
comic strip
above. The
cartoon
characters
were caught
in traffic
and unable
to make it
here on time.

10. Excuses, excuses ...

You might not think of yourself as a storyteller, but I bet if
there was something you didn't want to do you would be
able to come up with a good story about why you couldn't
do it. This type of story is called an 'excuse' and most of us
are really good at making them up when we need to.

An excuse may be true or completely made up. Having
an element of truth in your excuse helps to make it sound
more believable.

I have written quite a few stories that include or feature Andy coming up with ridiculously elaborate excuses. These include 'Go to bed!', 'I am a robot' and 'A really, really good excuse'.

In 'Go to bed!'—a story told completely in verse with footnotes—Andy comes up with every excuse he can possibly think of to avoid having to go to bed.

But Mum and Dad
ignore what I said.
'ANDY,' they say,
'JUST GO TO BED!'[16]

'But I've got a sore finger
and I've got a sore bum.
I've got pains in my legs
and my arms are all numb ...[17]

'Not to mention my lice
and my chronic back pain.
My cloudy vision!
My aching brain![18]

'My teeth! My tongue!
My eyes! My nose!
My tonsils! My kidneys!
My stomach! My toes![19]

[16]Okay, they asked for it ...
[17]None of this is true—I'm actually 100% healthy, but they don't know that.
[18]None of this is true, either—except for the lice.
[19]Actually, the more I think about it, the worse I feel.

It's not looking good.
They're tough nuts to crack.
But I WILL win.
I'm NOT going back.[32]

I'm going to give it
one last try.
It's time to pull out
My ultimate lie ...[33]

'But I CAN'T go to bed,'
I say to those two.
'I can't go now,
I've got homework to do!'[34]

'It's too late now,'
says my dad.
'Yes,' says Mum,
'it's just too bad!'[35]

[32]Not if I can think of another excuse, that is.
[33]I'm not saying it's good to lie, but sometimes parents leave you no choice.
[34]Well, actually, it's not a lie. I do have homework, but I have no intention of actually doing it.
[35]They obviously need a little more persuasion. Well, here it comes ...

'Go to bed!' from *Just Disgusting!*

In the story 'A really, really good excuse', Andy's excuse for being late for school is so elaborate that he has to sketch it out on the board to explain it fully. Andy's excuse is a ridiculous tale involving …

tight underpants,

attempted burglary,

being locked in a prison cell,

a notorious criminal,

a daring jail break,

an invitation to join an international crime ring,

an underpants-expanding machine,

a trial and then a police escort to school.

Just Shocking!

Unfortunately, it takes Andy so long to deliver his excuse that by the time he has finished, so has school and everybody has gone home, including the teacher.

In 'I am a robot', Andy tries to get out of doing household chores by pretending he is a robot.

'Neg-a-tive,' I say. 'It is not be-yond my cap-a-bil-it-ies. I am just not pro-grammed for it.'

'Well, how about helping me sort out this washing, then?' says Dad. 'It's the perfect job for a robot. Nice and repetitive. See? This sock goes with this sock. This sock goes with that sock.'

'Neg-a-tive,' I say. 'I am not a wash-ing sort-er-out-er ro-bot. I am not pro-grammed for that.'

'What's the use of a robot that can't do anything I ask it to do?' says Dad. 'Robots were invented to help people.'

'A-ffirm-a-tive,' I say, 'but ro-bots are not slaves. We have rights too. And be-sides, how can I make a cup of cof-fee if I am not pro-grammed to make a cup of cof-fee? It does not com-pute.'

'Hmmm,' says Dad, frowning.

'How about putting your head in the toilet and flushing it?' says Jen.

'Neg-a-tive. I am not pro-grammed for that,' I say. 'But I AM pro-grammed to put YOUR head in the toi-let and flush it.'

Just Shocking!

TRY THIS

Making up excuses

Choose one of the following items
and write down ten excuses for why
you are not able to do it.

- Go to bed
- Go to school
- Tidy your room
- Do your homework
- Finish this activity

... OR THIS

Conversation

Imagine somebody has just asked you to do
one of the things on the list above. Write a
conversation between the two of you in which you
come up with every possible excuse for why you
can't possibly do that thing. At the same time,
have the other person come up with a solution
for each of your excuses. Be as serious—or as
silly—as you like. (Note: the following example is
at the sillier end of the scale!)

ME: I can't sweep the floor.
ADULT: Why not?
ME: My leg is broken.
ADULT: Here, use this crutch!
ME: Gee, thanks ... but I have to go to school.
ADULT: No you don't.
ME: Why not?
ADULT: Because it's Saturday.

11. Explosions

I like explosions. Explosions are cool. And explosions that explode are even cooler. And exploding explosions that explode are even cooler still. And don't even get me started on exploding exploding explosions that explode! I guess it's no surprise that many of my books feature explosions and, luckily, Terry Denton is very good at drawing them.

A big fat cow exploding (*The Big Fat Cow That Goes Kapow*).

A fish exploding (*The 26-Storey Treehouse*).

A dog exploding after being treated by a very bad vet (*The Very Bad Book*).

A goldfish bowl exploding after being filled with oil and set on fire by bad Terence (*The Bad Book*).

Every living creature on Earth exploded.

Every living creature on Earth exploding in a story full of explosions ('The exploding butterfly story', *Just Shocking!*).

Santa exploding after being blown up by the bad baby (*The Bad Book*).

The bad baby exploding after playing with a hand grenade (*The Bad Book*).

The very bad dog plans a surprise for the cat (*The Very Bad Book*).

The cat exploding …

A fisherman exploding after being tricked by a very bad fish in *The Very Bad Book*.

Mr Big Nose's nose exploding (*The 13-Storey Treehouse*).

The Bum books (*The Day My Bum Went Psycho*, *Zombie Bums from Uranus*, *Bumageddon*) are full of things exploding. Here is just one of them—a giant pimple on Stenchgantor, the Great Unwiped Bum that helps to propel Eleanor and Zack to the next part of the story.

'No problem,' said Eleanor, opening her arms wide and pressing herself into the pimple. 'Pimple-climbing is a cinch.'

The pimple gave way to her body like it was made of plasticine. Using just the flat of her palm and her knees to create small indentations she was able to move surprisingly quickly up the pimple.

Zack opened his arms wide and jumped on. As he climbed he could feel the pimple juices squelching and shifting underneath him.

As they got towards the top, the pimple rounded out and sooner than expected, Zack found himself sitting on the top of the pus-packed summit with Eleanor.

'Are you ready?' said Eleanor.

'I guess so,' said Zack.

'Hold my legs,' said Eleanor.

She leaned down and wrapped her arms around the pimple, right under where Zack was sitting. She squeezed as hard as she could.

Zack felt the pus underneath him rise up like a big bubble but it remained trapped in the thin but rubbery pimple skin.

Zack searched his belt and found a set of sewing needles.

He took the largest and sharpest looking one out.

'This might help,' he said, and jabbed the needle into the top of the pimple.

It did help.

SHPLURRT!

The pimple burst like a geyser of hot molten cheese and Eleanor and Zack went shooting through the air towards the Sea of Bums.

The Day My Bum Went Psycho

TRY THIS

Draw something exploding

Imagine something exploding—your bedroom, your head, your teacher, your little brother or sister, your pet, etc.

What would it look like?

What type of things might come flying out of the explosion?

Draw and label your explosion.

Blood-sucking grannies exploding (*The Very Bad Book*).

12. Fast writing

One of the best ways I know to get ideas for writing is simply to start writing. I set a countdown timer for three minutes and start writing as fast as I can without stopping for the whole three minutes. If I don't have anything to write about I write about not having anything to write about ... It doesn't take long before I get sick of that and start writing about something more interesting.

I have to write an example of not being able to think of anything to write about for 'once upon a slime' but I can't think of anything to write about which is kind of weird when you think about it because I'm writing a whole book about what to write about so I should be able to think about a whole LOAD of things to write about but here I am just filling up a blank of sheet paper — oops, I mean blank sheet of paper with words about nothing about anything much because I can't think what to write about — ah! At last, the timer has gone off and my 3 minutes are up!

A piece I wrote in three minutes without stopping about not having anything to write about.

Sometimes I like to start with a random word like 'blue' or 'teeth' or 'tree' or 'dog'. I keep a whole bunch of random words in a bag beside my desk and use it like a lucky dip. We all have many stories inside us and sometimes all it takes is a single word to unlock them.

When I was growing up everybody just let their dogs run around the streets and they would be fighting with each other and chasing cars and pooping wherever and whenever they felt like it and nobody was running around with little plastic bags picking up after them. One dog, a beagle named Ricky used to sleep in the middle of the road. He got hit by a car and had to get his jaw wired up and after that his top jaw didn't quite match up with his bottom jaw which made him look kinda stupid. I remember Kerry, the girl whose dog it was, saying 'I can't wait until Ricky dies and then we can get a new dog that doesn't look so dumb.'

A piece of fast writing I wrote using the starting word 'dogs'.

Another way I like to start is with a phrase like 'I hate …' or 'I'm scared of …' or 'If only I …' or 'One of my favourite movies is …' or 'I remember …'

> I remember being a bit scared of escalators when I was little because I thought that your toes might get sucked into the top if you didn't jump off properly. I remember I couldn't wait to open a new box of cereal because they used to put a little plastic toy at the bottom. I remember how big and mysterious the pine forest at the end of our street used to seem. I remember our pet tortoise, Lucky, who used to escape on wet rainy nights. I remember how exciting it was when our grade 5 teacher, Mrs Jensen, brought a tape recorder in for us to play with. I used to record a comedy race call…('And chewing gum is stuck to the starting line…')

A piece of fast writing on the topic 'I remember …'

Many people ask me for tips on how to become a better writer. There is a lot of advice in this book, of course, but my number-one tip is to spend some time practising your writing every day and fast writing is an ideal way to do this. Begin with a modest goal of, say, five minutes a day and gradually increase from there.

I like to use simple, cheap exercise books so that I don't feel I have to write 'properly'. Unless I choose to read it to somebody it's for my eyes only—a place to play, experiment and be myself.

Not all writing is for publication. This is a stack of writing-practice journals I've filled over the years.

TRY THIS

Fast writing

Choose one of the statements or random words from the list on page 98. Write for three minutes without stopping. Don't think about what you're writing or try to edit or control it in any way. (You can edit it later—the point is to get words and ideas onto the page.) Be honest. See where the writing takes you. Tapping into your own experiences and emotions will give you all the ideas you will ever need.

Random phrases

- I hate ...
- I'm scared of ...
- I get annoyed by ...
- I love ...
- I believe ...
- I used to believe ...
- Yesterday, I ...
- I wish ...
- I was so embarrassed when ...
- The dumbest thing I ever did was ...
- What I really want to write about is ...
- I'll never forget ...
- If only I ...

- One of my favourite movies is ...
- I remember ...
- I'm proud of ...
- I'm not proud of ...
- I'm jealous of ...
- I'm happy when ...
- My favourite toy when I was young was ...
- When I daydream I ...
- My favourite place is ...
- I feel guilty when ...
- I like to be alone because ...
- I don't like to be alone because ...
- I would like to ...
- I am the one who ...
- The most dangerous thing I ever did was ...
- My faults are ...
- A time I learned from a mistake was ...
- A time I lied was ...
- My cousins are ...
- The worst thing about growing up is ...
- The last time I cried was ...
- The first time I ...

Random word fast-writing starters

Blue	Food	Legs
Teeth	Home	Eyebrows
Christmas	Pet	Beach
Birthday	Eyes	Park
Shoes	Football	Car
Sun	Ice-cream	Ear
Moon	Apples	Sock
Wind	Spying	Mud
Sunburn	Lunch	Water
Hats	Breakfast	Party
School	Cheating	Email
Ball	Summer	Bully
Fight	Toast	Key
Spider	Eggs	Skateboard
Dog	Cake	Bike
Cat	Band-aid	Accidents
Fish	Bed	Hospital
Friend	Sleep	Doctor
Grandma	Nightmare	Dentist
Grandpa	Dream	Vegetables
Brother	Bees	Fruit
Sister	Snake	Sand
Ghost	Desk	Pools
Tree	Book	Phones
River	Shorts	Holidays

13. Fun with food

I've always loved whipped cream and strawberries. In fact, when I was little, I loved them so much that I used to fantasise about filling up a room with whipped cream and strawberries and swimming around in it.

The whipped cream would be soft but thick enough to support my body and I'd imagine myself swimming around with my mouth open just sucking in strawberries and cream for the rest of my life.

It seemed perfect—well, as long as I didn't worry too much about how and where I'd go to the toilet, or whether the cream would go off after a while but hey, isn't *not* having to worry about practical considerations the whole point of a fantasy?

I used a version of this food fantasy in the story 'Why I love Choco-pops in fifty words or less' (*Just Shocking!*), except in this case Andy is imagining swimming around in a room full of Choco-pops and milk.

I know that a life spent swimming around in a room full of whipped cream and strawberries or Choco-pops and milk is maybe not everybody's idea of a good time, but one thing is for sure: fantasising about food is fun.

The Treehouse books are full of 'food fantasies'. For example, Andy and Terry have a marshmallow machine that follows them around and shoots marshmallows into their mouths whenever they are hungry. They also have a banana-enlarging machine and a machine that vaporises vegetables so they are in no danger of ever having to eat things like brussel sprouts.

When Andy and Terry make popcorn they leave the lid off and run around catching the freshly popped popcorn in their mouths. And when they need to quench their thirst, they do so in their lemonade fountain.

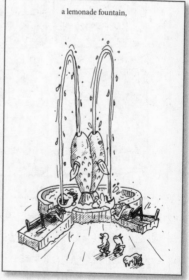

a lemonade fountain,

Andy and Terry eating popcorn and drinking lemonade treehouse-style.

They also have an ice-cream parlour with 78 flavours of ice-cream to choose from, including Goldfish Surprise, Flying Monkey and Deep-fried Doughnut.

The 26-Storey Treehouse

Of course, not all food fantasies are necessarily 'fun'. Sometimes they are deadly serious, such as when the bubbles Terry blows after drinking lemonade and chewing bubblegum are so large and so filled with burps that he becomes trapped in one and floats away from the treehouse.

Terry floating away from the treehouse in a burp-filled bubblegum bubble (*The 13-Storey Treehouse*).

Food can be used for things other than eating, of course: giant bananas are great for clearing your treehouse of unwanted monkeys.

The 13-Storey Treehouse

And, as Danny and Andy discover in the story 'Food fight' in *Just Stupid!*, almost any item of food can be used as a weapon.

DANGEROUS FOODS:

Sharpened banana.

Pineapple (radio-active).

A lit apple.

High altitude napalm strawberry.

Just Stupid!

USING A PINEAPPLE IN COMBAT.

Grasp in left hand.

Pull out pin with right hand and insert pineapple.

RUN!!

TRY THIS

Fantasy food machine

Design your own fantastical food machine. Draw a picture of it. Describe what it does, its features and any possible dangers associated with it. Feel free to use one of the ideas below.

A machine that:

- Can turn any type of food into chocolate
- Can make food come alive so you can play with it
- Can turn dirt into food
- Can make lollies invisible (so they are easier to hide)
- Can turn any type of food into a large cake (e.g. marshmallow cake, jellybean cake, bubblegum cake)

Marshmallow machine

... OR THIS

Food fight

Make a list of the ten best foods to use in a food fight. Use labelled diagrams to show how to use each food to attack others or to protect yourself against attack.

... OR THIS

Design a restaurant

Here's your chance to create the ultimate dining experience, either for yourself or for a specific type of customer. You can do it either as a description of what a typical visit to the restaurant might be like or you might find it easier to do it in the form of a labelled diagram, or a combination of both of these. Whichever way you choose, you will need to think about:

- The name of your restaurant
- The furnishings—tables, chairs, pictures, etc.
- The menu
- Is entertainment provided?

Themes for your restaurant might be:
- Sport
- Animals
- Exotic and unusual foods
- Completely imaginary foods
- Everything liquid
- Dangerous foods

Your restaurant could be for humans *or* it could be for:
- Dogs, cats, cows, etc.
- Aliens
- Zombies
- Vampires
- Witches

14. Graffiti

Almost as much fun as writing your own words and drawing your own pictures is playing around with words and pictures that already exist. There are many different ways to do this, but all involve a pen and a playful spirit.

This is my school diary from year 7. You can see that instead of using it to organise myself more effectively I was wasting time 'adjusting' the school's sporting code of behaviour.

A page from my year 11 school diary.

(b) **Code**

1. A ~~good~~ *bad* spirit is to be actively fostered between teams and between Schools, before, during and particularly after a game, *in brawls*.

2. Each game is under the control of the Umpire whose authority and decisions must *not* be respected. Abuse and intimidatory tactics must ~~not~~ be directed at the central umpire, *not* the goal umpires or the line umpires.

3. The Master-in-charge of each team is bound to insist that his players make the ball*s* their object. He will ~~not~~ allow such practices as the deliberate annoying or 'niggling' of a player by his opponent, especially when the ball*s* *are* in another section of the ground.

4. Spectators should ~~not~~ only barrack for their own team, but are *not* to show appreciation of good play or noteworthy effort by players in the opposing team. They must ~~not~~ barrack against their opponents ~~still less~~ direct unpleasant or belittling comments at the opposing team or at any player in that team. They must ~~not~~ stand inside the fence, or within five metres of the boundary of an unfenced playing field during the game. They may ~~not~~ converge on the teams during the breaks between the quarters.

5. The Master-in-charge of each team, or the Sportsmaster, or in the last resort, the Headmasters of the competing Schools, will draw the attention of spectators or of their own players to the points outlined in this Code, if, in their opinion, these are being ~~dis~~regarded during the games.

The original edition of *Just Tricking!* featured a trick book cover, *The Wonderful World of Freshwater Fish* by Sir Andrew Griffiths, which Andy, the main character of the book, has graffitied in an attempt to make the book his own.

The original *Just Tricking!* cover (1997)

The back cover blurb of the original *Just Tricking!* was supposed to look as if Andy had graffitied a library book about fish. Of course, no *actual* library book was harmed during the making of this cover.

The back cover also featured Andy adjusting the freshwater fish book blurb so that it was all about practical jokes instead of fish.

In the story 'A terrible Christmas and a crappy new year' (*Just Tricking!*), Andy intercepts the Christmas cards his sister is sending to her friends. He changes the greetings to be, well, a little less *Christmas-y* and draws all over the Santas' faces to make them, well, a little less *Santa-y* ...

Now for the greeting on the inside. Merry Christmas? I don't think so. I change the M on *Merry* to a T, cross out the Y and add IBLE to the end. And a happy new year? Not if I replace the H on *Happy* with CR. Much nicer . . . A TerrIBLE Christmas and a CRappy New Year.

I go through the rest of the cards, changing the greetings and adding eyebrows, scars, moustaches, nose-rings, eyebrow-rings, tattoos, antennae and Martian ears to the Santas. By the time I'm finished, no two Santas are alike. The only thing they have in common is that if you saw any of them coming towards you on the street, you'd turn and run the other way.

Just Tricking!

After he's posted them, though, he feels guilty about what he's done and suffers a terrible nightmare.

However, it turns out that Jen's friends love the punked-up Christmas cards and are inspired to make their own, including a heavy-metal Santa, a grunge Santa, a hip-hop Santa and a Frankenstein Santa.

TRY THIS

Graffiti some text and photos

Get a newspaper or a magazine that it is okay for you to graffiti over. Now perform the following series of tasks:

1. Turn the photo of one person into an alien.
2. Turn another photo of somebody into a zombie.
3. Add speech-bubble captions to both photos.
4. Adjust the headline and text of an article so its meaning is changed.
5. Find an advertisement and add speech bubbles to each person in it so they are saying that the product they are advertising is really terrible.
6. Add some zombies and aliens to the advertisement.

... OR THIS

Cut-up story technique

Take an article from a magazine and cut it up into random phrases, mix these together and then reassemble the article.

It probably won't make much sense but you may come up with some unexpected combinations of words and images that are funny or intriguing.

Make a list of your favourites.

Do they inspire a useful title? Or suggest an idea for a story?

Long ago many people were invented,
Others thought They dreamed like.

telescopes

the moon it was just another world.
what it was was really

the moon was a god. men saw
They wondered And some thought
a light in the sky. it was a
big ball of cheese!

15. I hate ...

I've written many stories featuring things I love, such as marshmallows, robots, explosions and time travel. On the other hand, I've also written many stories that include things I HATE, such as long queues in the post office, peeling off band-aids that have been left on for too long, trying to find a toilet in a multi-level shopping centre when you're busting, and don't even get me started on brussel sprouts ...

sprouts, I don't just mean I REALLY hate brussel sprouts, I mean I REALLY REALLY hate brussel sprouts.

And when I say I REALLY REALLY hate brussel sprouts, I don't just mean I REALLY REALLY hate brussel sprouts, I mean I REALLY REALLY REALLY REALLY REALLY REALLY REALLY REALLY REALLY REALLY hate brussel sprouts.

Who wouldn't hate them?

They're green.

They're slimy.

They're mouldy.

They're horrible.

They're putrid.

They're foul.

Apart from that I love them.

No, I don't. That was just a joke. There's absolutely NOTHING to love about brussel sprouts. Nothing at all. They're disgusting.

'Brussel Sprouts' (*Just Disgusting!*)

A great thing about things you—and/or your characters—hate is that you'll never run out of subjects to write about.

And chances are that you'll feel better for having made the effort to put your feelings into words. If your piece is read by others, it might make them laugh. Or cry. Or feel outrage on your behalf. Or perhaps it will simply reassure them that they're not the only ones who feel that way.

Many of the stories in the Just series are powered by Andy's endless rage against, well, practically everything!

18 Things Andy hates

1. Jeremy Smart
   ('I hate Jeremy Smart!', *Just Doomed!*)

2. School holidays
   ('I am a robot', *Just Shocking!*)

3. His annoying sister Jen
   ('In the shower with Andy', *Just Annoying!*)

4. Jen's annoying boyfriend, Craig
   ('Copycat from Ballarat', *Just Annoying!*)

5. Caravan holidays
   ('Shut-up!', *Just Disgusting!*)

6. Brussel sprouts
   ('Brussel sprouts', *Just Disgusting!*)

7. Trying to find a toilet in a multi-level shopping centre
   ('Busting', *Just Stupid!*)

8. Long queues in the post office
   ('Andy's Handbag', *Just Doomed!*)

ANDY'S GUIDE TO CRAIG BENNETT

① Pathetic, Gelled Hair.
② Primitive, Gorilla Eyebrows.
③ Dopey, nothing going on in the brain-Eyes.
④ Stupid- who'd want to kiss that-Mouth (liable to dribble in old age).
⑤ Neander-thal Shoulders.

9. Brown blobs in the bath
   ('Two brown blobs', *Just Disgusting!*)

10. His neighbour's scary garden gnome
    ('Wish you weren't here', *Just Annoying!*)

11. Sitting behind people with big hair at the movies
    ('The last Jaffa', *Just Annoying!*)

12. The Wiggles, his grade 4 teacher Mr Bradley,
    Macduff the garden gnome (*Just Macbeth!*)

13. Maths
    ('ANDY'S ACTION-PACKED MATHS PROGRAM!!!',
    Just Doomed!)

14. Babysitting his annoying little cousins
    ('Um-mah!', *Just Crazy!*)

15. Not winning the school short-story
    competition ('Kittens, puppies and ponies',
    Just Crazy!)

16. The sound of a snail being stepped on
    ('Snail aid', *Just Stupid!*)

17. Going to bed ('Go to bed!', *Just Disgusting!*)

18. Thinking you are a
    hero putting out a
    fire only to wake up
    to find you are actually
    dreaming and have
    wet the bed ('Busting',
    Just Stupid!)

TRY THIS

Make an 'I hate' list

Try writing a list of everything you hate—real things, imaginary things ... I don't care, as long as you hate them!

See if you can come up with at least five, and when you've got five see if you can come up with ten, and when you've got ten see if you can come up with twenty ... or more! (Don't you hate it when I keep pushing you like that?)

Be specific; don't just say 'chores', say exactly which chores you hate.

For instance, things you might hate could include:

- Certain types of weather
- A particular food
- The way some adults speak to kids
- Certain rules
- Annoying animals
- Music

... OR THIS

I hate, I REALLY, REALLY HATE!

Choose one of the things on your list of things you hate and, using the fast-writing technique on page 96, write about it in detail for at least five minutes.

Describe it in a way that makes your reader feel the same way you do about the thing you hate.

16. Illustrated stories

When I think back to the books I loved as a child—
for example, *The Cat in the Hat*, *Alice's Adventures in Wonderland*, *Winnie-the-Pooh* and *Coles Funny Picture Book*—I realise that I loved the illustrations as much as the stories. One of the reasons I love making books with Terry Denton is that he continually gives me great pictures that spark my imagination and inspire me to write stories to match them.

Illustrations can enhance and improve your stories in many ways. They can show where a story is set (e.g. the Treehouse series).

The 26-Storey Treehouse

Illustrations can show the action of the story (saving you the trouble of having to describe it).

The narrator of *The Big Fat Cow That Goes Kapow* (and his dog) being chased by Mike on his big spiky bike.

The journey taken by the head belonging to the boy who forgot to screw his head on (*The Very Bad Book*).

They help show what the characters in a story look like. And you can also use them to add funny incidents or characters that are not in the actual story (Terry does this a lot in the margins of the Just series and in the Treehouse books).

I'm hungry. I might eat some of these spare full stops.

gashes placed in his head ... or ... something unfortunate like that.

A little horse dining on some punctuation marks in *Just Macbeth!*

These rabbits are complaining about their pizza order, oblivious to the action of the story going on around them (*The 26-Storey Treehouse* is whizzing through the air above their heads).

A book?

I said 'extra carrot... don't you people ever listen?

Another important function of illustrations is to help make stories funnier through exaggeration.

The Bad Book

Also, illustrations can be the starting point for a story, rather than something that is added later. Once, when trying to get ideas for stories, I asked Terry what he liked to draw and he said, 'I really like drawing cows,' so I wrote the poem 'Big fat cows', which is how the book *The Big Fat Cow That Goes Kapow* came to be written.

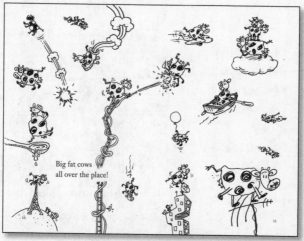

Terry loves to draw cows (*The Big Fat Cow That Goes Kapow*).

TRY THIS

Write an illustrated story

Ideas for illustrated stories:

- Retell a simple fairy tale or nursery rhyme
- Base a story on a recent school excursion
- Do an illustrated guide to your family
- Retell an incident from your childhood
- Base a story on something you like to draw

... OR THIS

Illustrated autobiography

Create an illustrated autobiography. In the example below, Terry has focused on the disgusting aspects of his life. You might like to write your own disgusting life story or you could pick another aspect of life as your theme, for example:

- My musical life story
- My action-packed life story
- My annoying life story
- My stupid life story

Terry's disgusting autobiography from *Just Disgusting*.

17. Incredible places

As a kid I used to love reading about incredible places—
Enid Blyton's magic faraway tree, Willy Wonka's chocolate
factory, the alien worlds described in horror comics and,
of course, the strange world that Alice discovered at the
bottom of a rabbit hole in *Alice's Adventures in Wonderland*.

As an adult I still love thinking up incredible places of
my own—crazy, wonderful places I would like to visit or
live in.

Here is a town
that is really incredible.
You can eat what you like
because
everything is edible.

Here is a sea
where you
can breathe
under water.

You can stay
under water
for an hour
AND a quarter.

Two of the incredible lands from *The Big Fat Cow That Goes Kapow*.

When I was young I was always a bit envious of kids who had treehouses. I loved the experience of climbing up into a tree and feeling like I was in a secret world. One day I asked Terry to draw a multi-level treehouse with a bowling alley and a tank full of man-eating sharks.

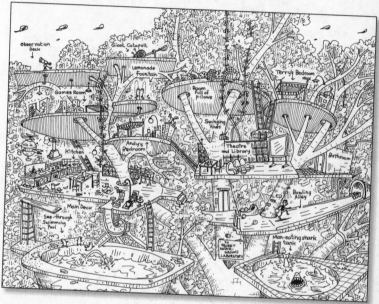

The 13-Storey Treehouse

As always, Terry added a whole lot of other stuff that I hadn't even thought about: a see-through swimming pool, a giant catapult and a lemonade fountain. I was pretty confident that this had to be the coolest treehouse in the world—until we added another 13 levels and created the 26-storey treehouse.

One of the fun things about the treehouse is that as well as being an incredible place in its own right, there are lots of incredible places within it.

THE MAZE OF DOOM: a maze so complicated that nobody who has gone in has ever come out again! (*The 26-Storey Treehouse*).

Incredible places can be places you'd like to live (e.g. the treehouse, the unusual lands shown in *The Big Fat Cow That Goes Kapow*), places nearby (e.g. inside a human body), places far away (other planets), places in other times (imaginary prehistoric places) even disgusting places (the world of the Bum novels).

While I would love to live in an amazing treehouse, I wouldn't necessarily want to live in all of the incredible places that Terry and I have created: for instance, the inside of a stomach doesn't look like much fun.

What Body Part is That?

TRY THIS

Draw an incredible place

Your place could be underground, underwater, in a tree, at the top of a tall tower: the sky's the limit. No, hang on, there *is* no limit! Your incredible place can be anywhere, even in space if you want.

Let your imagination run wild. Think of all the things you'd like around you, all the things you'd like to be able to do or see. Draw and label your incredible place.

... OR THIS

Write a travel brochure

Fold an A4 sheet of paper into three to make a brochure.

Imagine you are a travel agent and you have to write a 50–100 word description of your incredible place.

Try to make your incredible place sound as attractive as possible to any potential holidaymakers looking for the perfect spot for their next vacation.

Don't forget to include pictures.

How to kill a
KING

Drop a piano on him.

Drop an ocean liner on him.

Drop Jupiter on him.

Set a gang of squirrels on him.

18. Instructions & guides

The original version of the manuscript that was to become my first book, *Just Tricking!*, consisted of 200 practical (and not so practical) joke instructions. Eventually I expanded these into longer stories, but at first I found it easier to write them as if I was seriously instructing somebody how to play these very silly jokes.

Just Tricking!

A PRACTICAL (AND NOT SO PRACTICAL) JOKING GUIDE

Smell the cheese

Disguise your right hand as a block of cheese by making a fist. Then disguise your left hand as a plate by holding it out flat. Put the 'cheese' on the 'plate' and hold it up close to a friend's face and say, 'Would you like to smell the cheese?' When they say yes, tell them to put their nose on the plate and then, when they're having a nice big sniff, punch them in the nose. Then yell, 'JUST TRICKING!' and run away.

Potato pregnancy

Swallow a sack of potatoes and rush to the nearest hospital screaming, 'Help, I'm having a baby!' and then, after a long painful labour in which you scream a lot and run the doctors and nurses off their feet, suddenly pop the potatoes out all over the floor, yell, 'JUST TRICKING!' and run out of the birthing suite.

Fruit-salad fun

Chop yourself up into lots of little pieces and hide in a big glass bowl on the kitchen table so that you look exactly like a bowl of fruit salad. Wait until your family has eaten their main course, then heap yourself into each of their bowls and let them eat you. Then, when they've all finished, reassemble what's left of you and say, 'JUST TRICKING!— the fruit salad was ME and now you're all CANNIBALS and you're going to prison for EVER!'

An extract from the original *Just Tricking!* pocket book.

I particularly like using instructions to explain in ridiculous detail something that we all pretty much know how to do anyway (e.g. how to walk). Simple activities can be quite complicated when you think about it ...

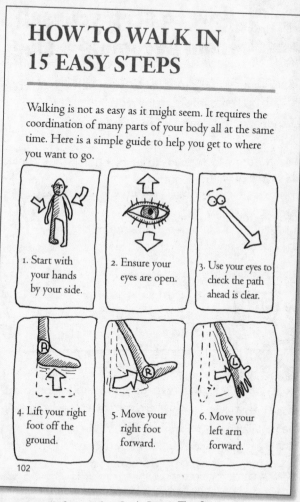

HOW TO WALK IN 15 EASY STEPS

Walking is not as easy as it might seem. It requires the coordination of many parts of your body all at the same time. Here is a simple guide to help you get to where you want to go.

1. Start with your hands by your side.

2. Ensure your eyes are open.

3. Use your eyes to check the path ahead is clear.

4. Lift your right foot off the ground.

5. Move your right foot forward.

6. Move your left arm forward.

102

'How to Walk' from *What Body Part is That?*

And, on the other hand, complicated problems can have quite simple solutions ...

SLUG MOON

How to stop yourself from becoming a slug

1. Scrub your skin vigorously with a Steelo soap pad every day to prevent slime from forming.

2. Sandpaper forehead daily to retard growth of unsightly horns.

3. Minimise intake of liquids to inhibit bubbling and foaming at the mouth.

4. Wear swimming goggles to prevent eyes from extending further than 2 cm from sockets.

5. Avoid watching television or hiding beneath bricks for long periods.

6. Do not eat more than one lettuce per meal.

7. Never ever accept a lift, dinner invitation or proposal of marriage from a slug.

8. Try to resist the temptation to eat slug bait, no matter how appealing it might seem.

9. Contact a pest-control expert if symptoms persist.

SLUG RODEO.

From one of my self-published pocket books 'How to Stop Yourself from Becoming a Slug'.

The margins of the Just books are crammed with Terry's helpful illustrated instructions on all sorts of subjects!

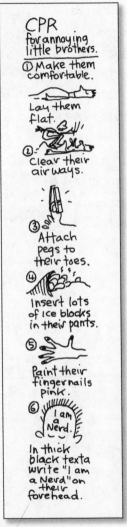

Just Stupid!

Just Stupid!

It's fun to pretend you are an expert on something. Terry and I have created two 'fact-free' guide books—*What Bumosaur is That?* and *What Body Part is That?*—in which the fictional narrator does his best to sound extremely knowledgeable while spouting complete nonsense. The key to this type of writing is not to *try* to be funny but to write in a very serious, very matter-of-fact tone as if it's all perfectly straightforward and unremarkable. I think it's this tension between the tone and the subject matter that many people have found so amusing ... and Terry's wonderfully 'realistic' illustrations, of course.

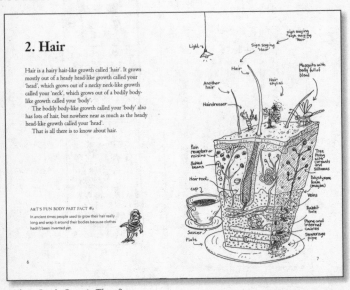

What Body Part is That?

138

It's also fun to write about one thing (e.g. a vacuum cleaner) as if it behaves like something completely different (e.g. an animal).

Terry is especially good at this sort of nonsense, as you can see from these examples.

Life cycle of a caravan (*Just Disgusting!*)

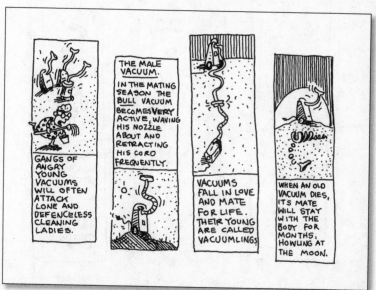

Vacuum cleaner facts (*Just Crazy!*)

Terry is also very good at producing guides to all sorts of natural phenomena and wildlife.

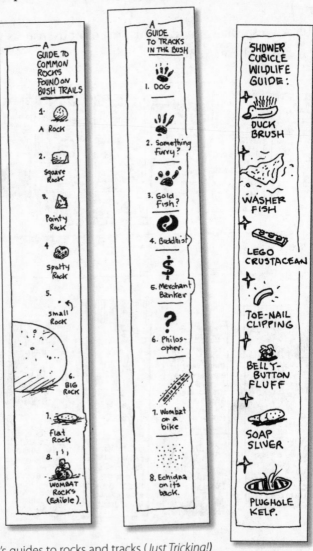

Terry's guides to rocks and tracks (*Just Tricking!*) and shower-cubicle wildlife (*Just Annoying!*)

TRY THIS

Write a serious guide to a ridiculous subject

Your guide could be a Facts About, a How To, a
Life Cycle or a list of types (e.g. What … is that?).
Just don't forget—you're the expert! Tell us
everything we need to know about your subject.
Illustrate it too, if you can.

Note: Your guide could be done in the form of a
pocket book (see page 223).

Feel free to use any of the following headings as
a starting point:

- How to be a real tough man
- How to be a real tough woman
- How to be a dog
- The life cycle of a moron
- Human beings: a user's guide
- What idiot is that?
- What teacher is that?

... OR THIS

Write a serious guide to a serious subject

Write a serious guide to a subject that you really do know about. For example:

- How to be a child
- A guide to my family
- How to look after a pet
- Football: A dummies' guide
- How to ride a horse
- What sport is that?
- What band is that?

19. I spy ...

Sometimes the easiest way to start writing is not to try to 'think something up' but simply to 'write something down'—and what better place to start than with what is right in front of your eyes?

My story 'The bad ant' is based on observation. I was outside one day with my notebook and pen and observed an ant going about its business (going up a blade of grass and down a blade of grass, etc.) and just wrote about what it was doing.

'The Bad Ant' from
The Bad Book

And the bad ant went along the ground and came
to a bit of grass. And the bad ant went up
the bit of grass. And the bad ant went over
the bit of grass. And the bad ant went
down the bit of grass.

grass

And then it stopped.

And then it started again.

Of course, the bit about the bad ant visiting Las Vegas, winning a million dollars and buying a red sports car and then running over an old lady was completely made up, but, hey, I had to do something to get the party started.

The point is that none of it would have happened if I hadn't had my notebook and my eyes open.

And the bad ant went to Las Vegas,

won ten million dollars

TIPPEE!

and bought a red sportscar.

Another story of mine based on observation is 'All the things I learned on the museum excursion last Tuesday'. This is based on two trips I made to the Melbourne Museum ... not to observe the exhibits but to observe school students interacting—or not interacting—with the exhibits.

The first thing I noticed is that kids really like pushing buttons!

I saw a boy walking around still wearing the 3-D theatre glasses, much to the amusement of his friends.

I overheard a teacher saying to her students outside the human body exhibit, 'Now, I expect a level of maturity here.'

(I don't think she got it!)

Though the story is based on observation, I must admit that I may have exaggerated some elements. For example, on the whole the museum guards seemed very friendly and helpful and I did not see any of them carrying weapons, let alone threatening to shoot anybody.

Just Doomed!

The thing is, when you write a story it doesn't have to be the same as real life ... which is a large part of the fun of writing stories!

TRY THIS

I can see ...

Write about what you can see right in front of your eyes. Whether it's your bedroom, a classroom, a garden, a busy street, a train carriage or even a quiet beach, all you have to do is start with the words 'I can see' and then write down what you see. Even if you think it's all too ordinary and obvious to be bothered writing about, write it down anyway. Some of the best writing is full of ordinary and obvious detail that everybody else is too busy to notice.

... OR THIS

Study something in super close-up detail

Brush up your observational skills. Look at something closely and try to describe it in as much detail as you possibly can.

Alternatively, you can make a close-up drawing. The idea is to look ... *really* look ... and notice.

Things to look at closely:

- A rock
- Your finger
- A leaf
- The carpet
- A flower
- A shoe
- The inside of a dog/cat's mouth
- The back of your hand

20. Jar labels

Did you know you can buy jars of vomit in the supermarket? Well, it's not really vomit. It's called 'corn relish' or 'mustard pickles' but it looks—and smells—exactly like vomit. What I like to do is to get a jar of corn relish, soak off the label and replace it with one of my own and give them to people as presents.

Andy's own
EMERGENCY
SPEW RELISH

FRONT LABEL

Andy's own

EMERGENCY SPEW RELISH

BACK LABEL

Of course, for my jar label to be really convincing it has to have all the elements of a real one: I have to tell the consumer how to use the contents of the jar and what the ingredients are.

Your bed is soft and warm. The last thing you want to do is to go to school. But can you convince your parents? What you need is Andy's own SPEW RELISH.

Directions for use
Spread generously around kitchen and bathroom surfaces. Tip some on your pillow and rub it into your hair for that 'I'm much too sick to go to school today' feeling!

Guaranteed pea-free and bile-enriched.

Warning: If swallowed, seek psychiatric advice.

Also Available: SNOT, STRAWBERRY JAM, EAR-WAX, TOENAIL CLIPPINGS and, soon to be available in aerosol cans: BAD BREATH.

9 781742 613048

My emergency spew relish has been very useful as a last-minute Christmas present over the years. It was also the inspiration for the story 'Emergency spew relish' in *Just Tricking!*, in which Andy attempts to gross out an old woman so she will no longer want to sit next to him on a plane. He uses the spew relish to pretend he's been sick and then makes a great display of eating it.

'Why certainly,' she says. 'Here you are.'

I take the teaspoon. This is it. Any minute now she'll be out of her seat like a rocket.

'Well, down the hatch.'

I open the neck of the sick bag and dip the spoon in. I scoop up a spoonful of spew relish and pull it out of the bag. I pass the spoon under my nose a couple of times and sniff deeply.

'Ahhh!' I say, smiling. 'I love it when it's nice and warm and fresh!'

I open my mouth very slowly. I put the teaspoon on my tongue and close my mouth. Then I slowly draw the teaspoon out and lick it clean, making sure I get every last drop. I close my eyes and sigh, as if I'm in heaven.

I open my eyes. I expect to see the seat next to me empty. I expect the old lady to be as far away from me as possible, and warning everybody else to stay away too.

But the seat is not empty.

The old lady is still there. Still watching.

'Was that nice?' she asks.

'It was beautiful,' I say. 'Tasted even better going down than it did coming up.'

'Emergency spew relish' from *Just Tricking!*

151

You can put almost anything into a jar and relabel it.

MUSTARD

SPAGHETTI

Andy's own

EAR WAX

Andy's own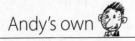

BRAINS

BACK LABEL

BACK LABEL

Nothing's worse than nagging parents: 'Clean up your room! Turn that noise down! Have you taken the rubbish out yet?' You know the sort of stuff. What you need is Andy's own EAR WAX.

Directions for use
Slap a couple of handfuls of Andy's own EAR WAX into each ear for that 'I haven't cleaned my ears for at least ten years!' feeling.

Complete oblivion to parental demands guaranteed or your money back.

Warning: Do not use Andy's own EAR WAX around dinner time as you will not hear parents calling you for dinner and may starve to death.

Also available in the Andy's own range: SNOT, FINGERNAILS, BELLY BUTTON FLUFF

Nothing's worse than realising the night before an exam that you haven't done any study. What you need is Andy's own BRAINS.

Directions for use
Remove lid. Rest head on table. Spoon Andy's own BRAINS into your ear until you feel more intelligent. The amount required will vary depending on the difficulty of the subject and how desperate you are.

Recommended dosage:
If you can't remember:
Important names/dates (1 tsp)
Maths formulae (2 tsp)
Anything—not even the name of the subject (whole jar)

Also available in the Andy's own range: COMMON SENSE, GENERAL KNOW-HOW, MECHANICAL APTITUDE

9 781742 613048

9 781742 613048

It doesn't have to be food-related—you can put almost anything into a jar and relabel it.

Andy's own

BOASTS

BACK LABEL

Nothing's worse than wanting to let the world know how good you are but running out of things to boast about because you've been too busy boasting about how good you are to actually do anything worth boasting about. What you need are Andy's own BOASTS.

Directions for use

Shake jar, open lid and pull out a boast. Read in a loud arrogant voice to anyone within earshot for that 'I'M BETTER THAN ANYBODY ELSE!' feeling. Repeat until you're surrounded by a large crowd worshipping you on their knees.

All boasts guaranteed vague and impossible to disprove or your money back!

We're not boasting but our BOASTS are the BEST IN THE WORLD!

Instructions

Write out each of the following BOASTS on a separate strip of paper and place the strips in a jar. (Feel free to make up your own boasts.)

'I'M THE BEST!'

'I'M THE GREATEST!'

'ANYTHING YOU CAN DO I CAN DO BETTER!'

'I DIDN'T EVEN STUDY AND I STILL GOT FULL MARKS!'

'I CAN RUN FASTER, JUMP HIGHER AND STAY UP LATER THAN ANYBODY ELSE IN THE WORLD!'

'I DON'T LIKE TO BOAST, BUT WITH ALL FALSE MODESTY ASIDE, GEE I'M GOOD!'

You can even put dirt and water into a jar and label it.

Andy's own

MUD

BACK LABEL

Nothing's worse than when you're out in the desert and you've got a craving for a good old-fashioned mud-pie. You're knee-deep in hot sand and there's not a raincloud or a clod of dirt in sight. What you need is Andy's own MUD!

Directions for use
Scoop out mud with hand and mould into the shape of a pie. Leave in the sun until cooked for that 'good mushy crunchy mud-pie' feeling!

Guaranteed 100% organic dirt (50%) and water (50%)

Also available: Andy's own SLIME, QUICKSAND, MOULD and SLUDGE

9 781742 613048

How to design a jar label.

Andy's own

MAGIC BEANS

YOUR BRAND →

YOUR PRODUCT →

INTRODUCTION →
'Are you sick of …
What you need is …'

DIRECTIONS →

GUARANTEE
(What is your product
guaranteed to do, or
what makes it better
than any other
competing product?)

WARNING
(What's the worst
thing that could
happen?)

ALSO AVAILABLE
(Related products)

BARCODE & NUMBER →
(For extra realism)

Are you sick of having an old cow and no money to buy food?

What you need is Andy's own MAGIC BEANS!

Directions for use
Throw a handful of beans onto the ground before going to bed. Wake up in the morning, climb the giant beanstalk, steal the giant's golden goose and then chop the beanstalk down before the giant can catch and/or eat you.

Guaranteed to grow a giant beanstalk overnight or your old cow back!

WARNING: Do not swallow as a giant beanstalk may grow up your neck and out of your mouth, nostrils and ears.

Also available: MAGIC WANDS, MAGIC DUST, MAGIC POTION

9 781742 613048

TRY THIS

Make a jar label

Put something interesting into a jar. (If you don't actually have a jar you can still make a label for an imaginary jar.)

Make a label for the front and back of your jar. Think about including the following on your labels: an introduction to your product, directions for its use, a list of ingredients, warnings, guarantees, other related products you have in your range, and—of course—a barcode.

You can also include persuasive words to attract the consumer's attention:

21. Just terrifying!

We are all scared of something, whether it's the bogeyman who lives under the bed, the thought of having your toes sucked into the top of an escalator, or maybe it's the sight of a severed arm crawling across the bedroom floor towards you in the middle of the night.

In the Schooling Around series there is a character called Newton Hooton who is terrified of EVERYTHING: spiders, busy roads, heights, lightning, cotton buds, butterflies. You name it, Newton is scared of it ... especially lions!

Principal Greenbeard continued to speak. 'Now I don't wish to alarm you,' he said, 'but we've just been notified that a circus lion has escaped and there have been several sightings that indicate the lion is heading in our direction at an alarming rate of knots. I would just like to warn all crew members to stay inside and keep all cabin doors and portholes fully secured. I repeat, batten down all hatches until further notice. Thank you all, and please remember that it's very important that we do not panic.'

The PA speaker fell silent.

People started panicking.

Some students screamed.

Some students jumped up on their chairs.

Some students screamed and jumped up on their chairs.

But nobody screamed louder than Newton.

'Aaaaagggghhh!' he wailed. 'I'm scared of lions!'

'You're not the only one,' said Gretel. 'We're all scared of lions!'

'No, you don't understand!' said Newton. 'On my top ten list of things I'm scared of, lions take up nine places!'

Pencil of Doom

In contrast to Newton Hooton is Brave Dave, a character who is apparently scared of nothing ... or is he?

This is Dave who,
during the day, is really,
really,
REALLY brave.

But, during the night,
when there's no light,
Dave is NOT brave.
He takes fright.

Each noise he hears
increases his fears.
Every bump,
every thump,
makes his poor heart JUMP!

He sucks his thumb.
He calls for his mum.
He can't wait
for the morning to come.

So, if you need
a brave job done,
call Dave in the day ...

But at night,
call his mum.

'Brave Dave' from *The Big Fat Cow That Goes Kapow*

Sometimes the most seemingly unterrifying things can be the most terrifying of all. My sister Julie had a garden gnome whose head had been knocked off and then glued back on, so it looked like it had a huge gash in its neck. It also had a slightly evil-looking face and Julie admitted to me once that she found it scary. I found the idea of someone being frightened of a small concrete statue very funny and decided to write a story about an 'evil' garden gnome ('Wish you weren't here', *Just Annoying!*).

broken hat

beady eyes

severed head

beardy beard

bad knees

dirty toenails

missing nose

creepy smile

What's this—a gnome bag? What's he got in it—a gnome gun?

no shoes

Julie's 'evil' garden gnome.

P.S. I also find over-labelling illustrations rather amusing.

Andy (as Macbeth) fighting Macduff, the garden gnome, in *Just Macbeth!*

TRY THIS

Write a list of scary things

Write a list of scary things (they can be real or imagined). After each one try to briefly explain what it is that makes that thing so particularly scary.

You can use the things you are scared of to bring real energy to your writing and to connect with your reader because the chances are that they are scared of exactly the same things you are.

If you have time, present your list as a comic strip or pocket book.

Feel free to use the list below to help jog your memory:

- Speaking in public
- Insects and bugs
- Dogs
- Darkness
- Heights
- Deep water
- Flying
- Escalators
- Elevators
- Spiders

According to Jill in *The 26-Storey Treehouse*, even spiders are scared of spiders.

... OR THIS

How to scare ...

Choose a person from the list below and write a short guide explaining how to scare them.

- Mother
- Father
- Brother
- Sister
- Grandparent
- Babysitter

- Teacher
- Neighbour
- Bus driver
- Museum attendant
- Police officer
- Shop assistant

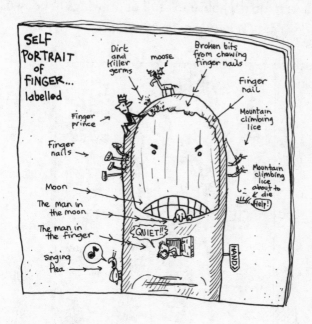

22. Labelled diagrams

One of the (many) great things about working with Terry is that he is really good at drawing labelled diagrams. One day, I said, 'Terry, draw me a finger, please,' and instead of just drawing some boring old finger, he came up with this!

I mean, the man is clearly a genius. I liked it so much I said, 'We have to do a whole book full of drawings of body parts,' and so we did (*What Body Part is That?*).

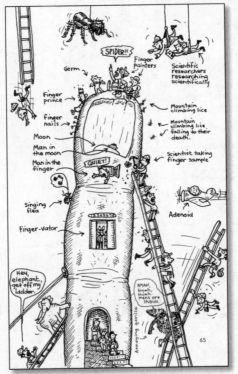

Terry's incredibly informative diagram of a finger from *What Body Part is That?*

You can use diagrams to do things like show the inside of something, the path something took, how something works or how to make or do something. Diagrams can also be combined with instructions, lists, stories—any piece of writing, really.

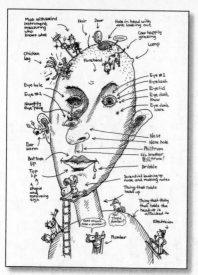

Terry's diagram of a face from *What Body Part is That?*

Some useful information about brains from *The 13-Storey Treehouse*.

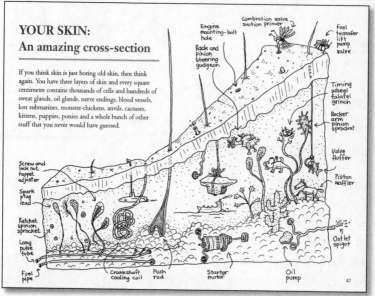

What Body Part is That?

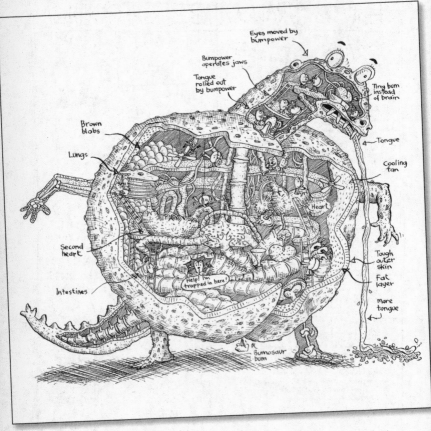

A labelled diagram from *What Bumosaur is That?* showing the internal workings of a bumosaur.

How To DRAW A LABELLED DRAWING

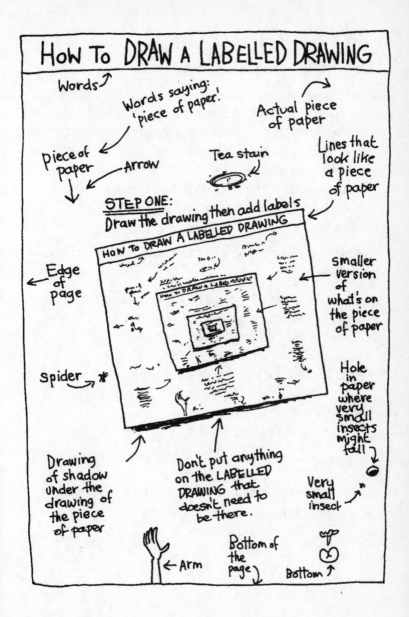

Words ↗

Words saying: 'piece of paper!'

Actual piece of paper

Piece of paper ←   → Arrow

Tea stain

Lines that look like a piece of paper

STEP ONE:
Draw the drawing then add labels

HOW TO DRAW A LABELLED DRAWING

Edge of page

Smaller version of what's on the piece of paper

spider → *

Hole in paper where very small insects might fall

Drawing of shadow under the drawing of the piece of paper

Don't put anything on the LABELLED DRAWING that doesn't need to be there.

Very small insect

← Arm

Bottom of the page ↘

Bottom ↗

TRY THIS

Draw a labelled diagram

Choose a subject and draw a labelled diagram to explain it. Choose something you know about or something you don't know about but would like to pretend you are an expert on. (Don't ever let not knowing about something stop you from being an expert on it.) Your diagram can be serious and realistic or as silly as you can make it.

Some ideas for those having trouble getting started:

- A cross-section or bird's-eye view of what goes on in each room of your house on an average weekday morning/evening or Saturday/Sunday morning
- A labelled diagram of a member of your family (or the whole family)
- How a dog's body works
- How a cat's body works
- A family tree

Note: maps are a particular type of labelled diagram—see Map-making, page 185 for more ideas.

23. Lifting the lid

If you stumbled across a mysterious box that was clearly labelled KEEP SHUT, you'd just mind your own business and walk right past, wouldn't you? Yeah, right! Like most of us, you'd stop and lift the lid just to see what's in there.

A fun way to get started writing is to draw somebody opening a locked box and then to write a sentence or two about what comes out. Here are a few examples that Terry and I came up with.

I opened the box and I immediately wished I hadn't.... it was my dad's moth collection and I was pretty sure I wasn't going to be able to get them all back in before he got home.

But I did... I just did... and I'm so glad because out jumped the **ADORABLEST** puppy in the WHOLE WORLD.

TRY THIS

Lifting the lid

Draw a picture of a character or yourself lifting the lid on a container clearly labelled KEEP SHUT. There is absolutely no way of predicting what might be inside or why it was shut in there. It could be:

- The most horrible thing imaginable
- A wonderful surprise
- Somebody you haven't seen for a long time (friend or enemy)
- Something you lost a long time ago

Write a short piece of text underneath your picture explaining what has happened and how the character feels about their discovery.

The completed pictures could be collected, photocopied and made into an entertaining 'Lifting the Lid' book.

... OR THIS

Time machine

You are out taking a ride in your time machine when you are sent spinning out of control by a freak time-storm. Finally the time machine stops moving. You have no idea where you are or what day, year or century you are in—you could be anywhere, any time.

Create a 'snapshot' picture of the scene that greets you when you open the door of your time machine. After you have finished drawing, write a short piece of text (no more than three or four sentences) to accompany it.

You might like to start it with the sentence, 'The first thing I saw when I opened the door of my time machine was ...'

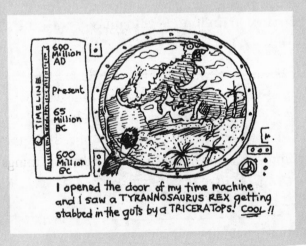

I opened the door of my time machine and I saw a TYRANNOSAURUS REX getting stabbed in the guts by a TRICERATOPS! COOL!!

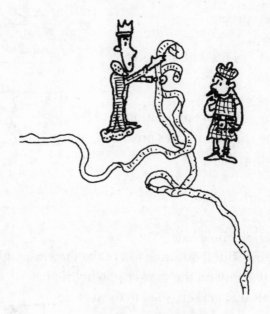

24. Lists

Before I began writing *Just Disgusting!* I made a list of disgusting ideas to write stories about. One day I was reading the list aloud to a group of students to see which topics interested them the most and I noticed that they were simply enjoying having a list of disgusting things read out to them. I figured that if I made it long enough (e.g. 101 entries), then the list itself could be a story.

101 Really Disgusting Things

1. Brussel sprouts.
2. Maggots.
3. Brussel sprouts with maggots in them.
4. Picking your nose.
5. Picking your nose and eating it.
6. Picking somebody else's nose and eating it.
7. Scabs.
8. Scabs with maggots.
9. Maggots with scabs.
10. Shower-plughole hair.
11. The slimy stuff that comes out of the shower-plughole when you pull on the shower-plughole hair.
12. Animals that get squashed in the middle of the road and then get run over a whole lot of times until they're just disgusting red blobs.
13. Dog poo.
14. Accidentally standing in dog poo and getting it on the bottom of your shoe.
15. Getting dog poo on your fingers when you're trying to get the dog poo off the bottom of your shoe.

Just Disgusting!

Lists are a good way to have fun with an idea without having to write a whole story about it. I find that when you have one idea it often suggests another ... and another ... and another ...

A list of ten of the lists in my books

1. 101 really disgusting things (*Just Disgusting!*)
2. 101 really dangerous things (*Just Shocking!*)
3. 101 ways to be doomed (*Just Doomed!*)
4. Mr Shush's top ten list of things you should never do to a library book (*Robot Riot!*)
5. Ten pieces of evidence that prove beyond a doubt that Roberta is a robot (*Robot Riot!*)
6. Newton Hooton's top ten list of things he is scared of (*Pencil of Doom!*)
7. Terry's extremely long 'to do' and 'to don't' lists (*The 13-Storey Treehouse*)
8. The top 5 dumbest things Terry has ever done (*The 26-Storey Treehouse*)
9. Worse things than being a pirate (*The 26-Storey Treehouse*)
10. A list of ten of the lists in my books (*Once upon a Slime: 45 Fun Ways to Get Writing ... Fast!*)

Falling Sharks, no. 93 in '101 really dangerous things'.

The 26-Storey Treehouse

Writing a list of ten things you should know about someone or something is one of my favourite list activities. It's always good to have a set number of things to write because it forces you to rise to the challenge and in the process come up with ideas that might not have occurred to you otherwise.

Ten things you should know about my dad

1. Can't have a cup of tea without a biscuit.
2. Takes ten times longer than any other human to eat his meal.
3. Can't stand a mess outside the laundry door.
4. Hates dirty tissues.
5. The smellier the cheese, the more he likes it.
6. Exceedingly cheery at 6.30 a.m.
7. Doesn't mind a beer.
8. Barracks for Collingwood.
9. Won't take no for an answer when offering food or drink.
10. Can wiggle his ears.

I like doing these lists so much that sometimes it's hard to stop at ten …

Ten MORE things you should know about my dad

1. All his attempts to imitate foreign accents sound the same.
2. Wears a cool yellow safety helmet at work.
3. Says sorry to doors and walls when he bumps into them.
4. Owns the oldest and crappiest trailer in the world.
5. Makes great birdbaths.
6. Has trouble remembering the gender of dogs and cats.
7. Hates computers.
8. Not afraid to use the jokes that others reject.
9. Always hears if you sneak in late at night.
10. Loves meringues.

Terry also likes doing illustrated lists, as you can see from these examples.

Just Shocking!

Just Shocking!

Just Stupid!

Just Stupid!

TRY THIS

Write a list (illustrate it if you like)

The great thing about lists is that they can be about anything—you can list favourite stuff, things you hate, rules you've broken, places you've been, things you'd like to do when you're older, things you'd like for Christmas, things you don't want for Christmas.

Or you could write a 'ten things' list about someone you know well—your mum, dad, grandma, grandpa, pet, best friend, or favourite book or TV character.

If you don't want to write a list, then just write down ten things you'd rather be doing than writing a list.

TEN THINGS YOU COULD WRITE ABOUT IN YOUR 'TEN THINGS YOU SHOULD KNOW ABOUT' LIST

1. Football
2. Horses
3. Music
4. Computers
5. Movies
6. Books
7. Bikes
8. Skateboards
9. Food
10. Dogs

I THINK I'LL DO HORSES … OR MAYBE SKATEBOARDS

Oh, look, I've written another list!

... OR THIS

Write a TO DO list ... write a TO DON'T list

Make a list of all the things you HAVE to do in a typical week. Now make a list of all the things you would LOVE to do instead. Combine both lists to create your ultimate TO DO list.

Now, create your ultimate TO DON'T list.

The 13-Storey Treehouse

25. Map-making

I was pretty good at making really authentic treasure maps when I was at school. After drawing them up I would give them that all-important authentic hundreds-of-years-old look by staining them yellow with tea and then carefully burning the edges. (Sometimes I'd do it not so carefully and I'd accidentally set the whole map on fire and have to start all over again.) I love the idea of treasure maps and buried treasure so much that I wrote a whole book about them called, appropriately enough, *Treasure Fever!*

Burying treasure wasn't the only thing I enjoyed doing. Here's a map of the neighbourhood I grew up in that shows some of my other favourite ways to amuse myself.

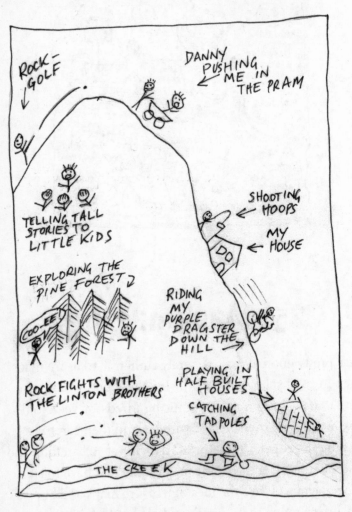

Andy's play map (drawn by Andy, NOT Terry, in case it's not obvious).

You can make a map of almost anything! In *The 13-Storey Treehouse* there's a map showing Silky the flying cat's journey through the sky.

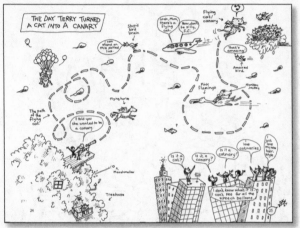

The 13-Storey Treehouse

Here's a map showing what could happen if a rocket went out of control and travelled all over the universe.

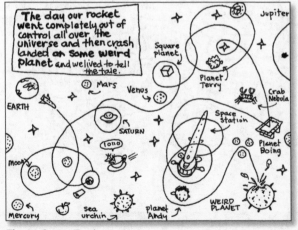

The 39-Storey Treehouse

You can even make a map of your own brain—or someone else's.

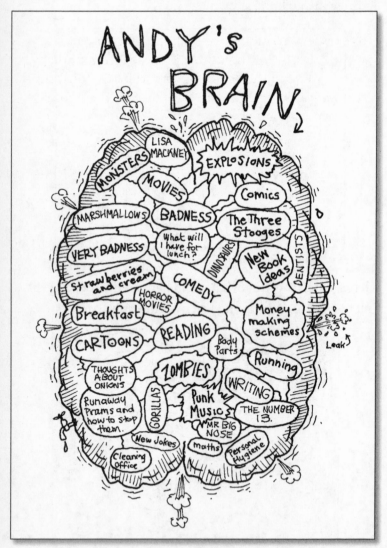

A map of the inside of my brain (according to Terry Denton).

TRY THIS

Map a real place

Draw a map of your neighbourhood (not to scale) highlighting places that are important to you. You could include places where something memorable happened, for example, the place where you had your worst bike accident, or places you go regularly, like your school and your best friend's house. Indicate how important the thing is to you by making it bigger than other places on the map.

Ideas for maps:

- A map of all the places where you've had accidents

- A play map showing all the places where you've played

- A map of all the places you would typically visit in one week

- A map of your favourite places to get food

- A map showing a recent trip and highlights along the way (e.g. interstate, to your grandparents, a bike ride)

... OR THIS

Map a journey or an imaginary place

Imagine you've just done the most amazing kick of a football ever. Show the progress of that football as it leaves your foot and takes off into the world. Don't forget to include the reactions of humans and animals as the football passes by.

Draw a map titled 'The day my boomerang wouldn't come back' and show the boomerang's path.

If you are writing a story, draw a map showing the place (or places) the story is set. This will improve your storytelling as it makes you think about the physical details of your story and helps you to visualise things more clearly.

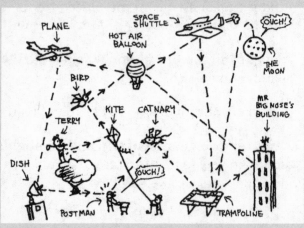

Map showing the day Terry hit a golfball to the moon.

26. Monsters, aliens, robots & zombies

The first (and still the most terrifying) monster I ever encountered in books was the dreadful Jabberwock (pictured above) in Lewis Carroll's *Through the Looking-Glass and What Alice Found There.*

In *The 13-Storey Treehouse* Andy and Terry are terrorised by a hideous sea monster. (Note: Any similarity between the Jabberwock and Mermaidia the sea monster is entirely deliberate!)

Mermaidia scaring Andy and Terry (*The 13-Storey Treehouse*).

Just Disgusting!

In 'The story of the very stupid boy and the very big slug', Danny creates a giant slug for his school science project. The 'super slug' breaks free of Danny's garage where he has been force-feeding it cans of dog food and begins to devour the entire world.

Luckily, Andy has been working on a time machine for his project and is able to use it to go back in time and convince Danny not to create a giant slug by telling him 'The story of the very stupid boy and the very big slug'. By doing so, Andy not only saves the world but also impresses the girl he loves. Yeah, I know it's stupid … but it's SO much fun!

When I was young I loved reading American horror comics. They were full of crazy stories about mad scientists, invading aliens, monsters and zombies. These provided a rich source of inspiration for the Bum trilogy.

I also loved books about dinosaurs, which came in handy when Terry and I began creating the bumosaurs for *What Bumosaur is That?*

Stink Kong from *What Bumosaur is That?* and the giant gorilla in *The 13-Storey Treehouse* were both inspired by *King Kong*, one of my favourite movies (the original 1933 one, that is, though the 2005 remake is pretty darn good too!).

The giant gorilla from *The 13-Storey Treehouse*.

The giant gorilla fighting flying cats (*The 13-Storey Treehouse*).

Stink Kong (*What Bumosaur is That?*)

The idea for *Killer Koalas from Outer Space* came from talking to a group of children in America. I was talking about koalas and they asked if they were dangerous. Well, I couldn't help myself: I told them that, of course, they were *extremely* dangerous and that it was quite common in Australia for people to have their faces ripped off by the long, sharp claws of a koala. They weren't quite sure whether to believe me but I enjoyed telling this story so much I decided to write it. I knew, however, that Australian children would know koalas were definitely not *that* dangerous, so I made the koalas aliens because *nobody* knows how dangerous koalas from another planet would be!

Killer Koalas from Outer Space is a collection of stories from *The Bad Book* and *The Very Bad Book*.

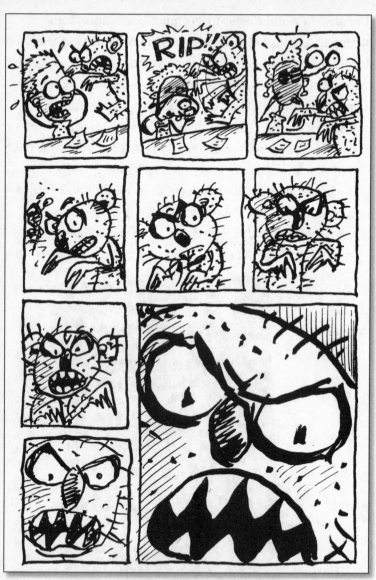

'Killer Koalas from Outer Space' (from *The Very Bad Book*).

I've always found the word 'zombies' and, indeed, the whole idea of zombies quite amusing. As a result, quite a few of my books and stories feature zombies, for example, 'Sleepover of doom' in *Just Doomed!*

Zombie

Andy's head

You drive into the cemetery. A bunch of brain-eating zombies are having a dance party. You smash right into the middle of them. They scatter like bowling pins, except for one who ends up on the roof of your car. He's banging on the roof yelling, 'Brains! Brains! I want brains!' The poor zombie doesn't realise that, between the pair of you, Danny and yourself barely have two brain cells to rub together. But without ripping your heads open he can't possibly know that. So he keeps pounding and pounding and yelling for brains while you keep swerving the car from side to side, trying to shake him loose.

'Sleepover of doom' from *Just Doomed!* is a choose-your-own adventure story featuring zombies.

TRY THIS

Create a monster

It can be a lot of fun thinking up terrifying creatures or scenarios. But don't just take my word for it—try it for yourself. Think up a horrible, disgusting, vile, vicious, life-threatening monster of some sort. It could be an alien, or a life-form we are familiar with that has been horrifically mutated, or it could be a completely alien creature from another planet.

Describe your monster. Illustrate it (if you dare!) and label its most destructive features.

... OR THIS

Mix and match

Mix and match the words from the columns below to come up with your own monster (you can use more than one adjective to describe your noun). Draw it. Describe it. And then get out of there fast before it kills you!

Adjective	Noun
Killer	Kangaroo
Mutant	Koala
Zombie	Wombat
Blood-sucking	Cockatoo
Crazy-eyed	Platypus
Abominable	Granny

27. Mr Scribble cartoons

Mr Scribble—one of Terry's most popular cartoon characters—appears in the marginal cartoons in the Just series. For such a simple character (after all, he is just a bit of scribble), Mr Scribble leads a very active life. For example, he goes surfing, rollerblading, shopping for bagels, dresses up for the opera and even buys a missile at one point.

A small sample of the many adventures of Mr Scribble.

Just Annoying!

Just Annoying!

Just Annoying!

Just Disgusting!

Just Shocking!

Just Doomed!

Just Shocking!

Just Shocking!

Just Shocking!

Just Shocking!

Just Stupid!

TRY THIS

Draw your own Mr Scribble cartoon

The best thing about Mr Scribble is that he is very easy to draw. All you have to be able to do is scribble.

Think up your own title or use one from the list below:

- Mr Scribble goes skydiving
- Mr Scribble has a bath
- Mr Scribble goes skateboarding
- Mr Scribble's day at the beach
- Mr Scribble's birthday party
- Mr Scribble falls in love

END OF WORLD

An unconfirmed report has come in that the universe has blown up, and every creature in it has been killed. We don't know whether this is so or not. We shall let you know as soon as we know ourselves.

28. Nutty news

'End of World' is my favourite ever fake news article. It comes from *Cole's Funny Picture Book No. 3*, which was one of my favourite books when I was growing up. One of the funniest pages in the book was a make-believe newspaper called *Animail: All the news of the Jungle*. It was full of stories about snakes swallowing themselves, missing elephants and mosquito egg-laying competitions.

Writing fake news articles is something I really like to do, as you can probably tell from the following examples.

Cow in orbit!

A Jersey cow is still in orbit after becoming the first cow in the history of the world to jump over the moon last night.

Miss Daisy Bell is believed to be orbiting the earth at 300 kilometres per hour. Authorities are currently looking at ways to pull her back to the ground.

It is rumoured that the current world lasso champion, Wild Bill Burley, has been called in to help.

Miss Daisy jumped from the top of a barn in a paddock south-east of Leongatha, a small farming community in Victoria.

An eyewitness said her jump was accompanied by a cat who played the theme from *Rocky* on a fiddle.

Miss Daisy is a founding member of the daredevil group, The Jumping Cows Society.

A spokesbull for the society, Mr Heifer, was over the moon about the jump.

'It's a big leap for a cow, and an even bigger leap for cow-kind,' he said. 'We are all very proud of Miss Daisy. It was a fine effort, especially when you consider that she weighs over 500 kilograms and had a full udder. We just hope that she will be able to get back down safely.'

Aside from the high jump, other activities of the society include cow parachuting, bull bungee-jumping and heifer hang-gliding.

The activities of the Jumping Cows have been strongly opposed by Farmers Against Farm Animals Doing Stupid Things. The president of the group, Mr Bob Sensible, warned that stronger measures would be taken to keep cows in their paddocks where they belong.

'This jumping nonsense has gotten out of hand. Cows have to realise that they are not birds. They are ground-dwelling mammals and their job is to stand quietly in a paddock, chew grass and make milk.'

Student's brain explodes during maths test

The strain of a maths test became too much for year 9 student Daniel Pickett, whose brain exploded during a maths test yesterday.

'I could see him struggling on the first page,' said a friend. 'He was just shaking his head and muttering stuff like "I don't get this" over and over again.'

Police investigating the scene believe that it may have been a three-part question involving inverse functions that caused the explosion.

'He obviously tried to work it out in his head instead of using a calculator,' said Chief Inspector Smartypants. 'You shouldn't try to do that unless you're either crazy or very clever, like me.'

School cleaners were furious. 'Teachers set tests of this difficulty with no consideration for the people who have to clean up afterwards,' said a union official. 'If it happens again we may consider some sort of action.'

The maths teacher, however, was unrepentant. 'I don't care how many students' brains explode,' said Mrs Ten-out-of-ten. 'Maths is an important life skill and my students are going to learn it even if it kills them—which, in the case of Daniel, it obviously did.'

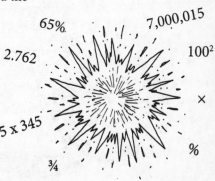

An artist's impression of what Daniel Pickett's brain exploding would have looked like.

I Grew Legs! Tadpole Tells

A tadpole has revealed how its life was dramatically changed when it lost its tail and grew legs.

'At first I felt pretty stupid,' said the tadpole, who was one of many tadpoles collected for study in the grade 4 science class a few weeks ago.

'I mean, I'd never had legs before and I just didn't know what to do with them—I was slipping and falling all over the tank.

'I don't know why it happened to me. Up until then I'd been playing chasey, doing laps and eating as much as I could, just like everybody else.

'I guess in the back of my mind I'd always known that growing legs was a possibility but I never thought that it would happen to me.'

The tadpole is uncertain as to what the future holds for him. 'I'm not sure where to go from here. There are plenty of rumours; some say you become a frog or even a student, but I reckon they're just pulling my leg—I mean, can you imagine anything worse?

'I've had a few offers from running clubs and dance companies but I think I'll just wait and see—I'd rather stay in the tank with all my friends if I can.'

A fake TV news flash from *The Very Bad Book*.

These 'Daily Bad News' articles are from 'A really, really good excuse' in *Just Shocking!*

I GASPED. IT WAS SQUIZZY 'TEASPOON' TAYLOR, A CRIMINAL MASTERMIND FAMOUS FOR DIGGING HIS WAY OUT OF HIGH-SECURITY PRISONS ALL OVER THE WORLD USING NOTHING BUT A TEASPOON!

⊗ DAILY BAD NEWS
SQUIZZY 'TEASPOON' TAYLOR DIGS OUT OF JAIL AGAIN

NOW THE SITUATION WAS *REALLY* SERIOUS!

⊗ DAILY BAD NEWS
SITUATION REALLY SERIOUS

TRY THIS

Write a news article

Take your favourite nursery rhyme, novel, song or movie and write it up as if it were big news.

A newspaper article should answer the five 'W's.

1. What happened?
2. Who was involved?
3. Why did it happen?
4. When did it happen?
5. Where did it happen?

A sixth question, 'How did it happen?', can be dealt with in more detail once these five essentials have been answered.

Try to get an interesting angle on your story by deciding on the most newsworthy item. For instance, in the 'Hey Diddle Diddle' rhyme there are many possible angles you could tell the story from. Here are a few: Spoon carried off by dish. Cow jumps over moon. Little dog laughs. Cat plays fiddle.

29. Once upon a slime

Nursery rhymes and poems have always been a great source of inspiration and amusement to me. They are full of wonderful plots and crazy characters, and the best part is that you are free to borrow from them to create your own stories.

Bad Diddle Diddle

Bad diddle diddle
   The cat did a piddle
The cow did a poo on the moon.
    The little dog barfed to see such fun
      And then ate it all up with a spoon.

Very Bad Mary, quite contrary,
How does your garden grow?
With poison ivy, prickles and thistles,
And spiky weeds all in a row.

Mary Had a Very Bad Lamb

Mary muttered to herself,
'This really will not do!'
And so she shot and killed the lamb
And had a baa-becue.

Mary had a very bad lamb,
Its fleece was black as tar.
It smoked and drank and stayed up late
At its favourite all-night baa.

It followed her to school one day
In its bright-red Lamb-borghini,
Wearing nothing but a sheepish grin
And Mary's new baa-kini.

My bad versions of nursery rhymes from
The Bad Book and *The Very Bad Book*.

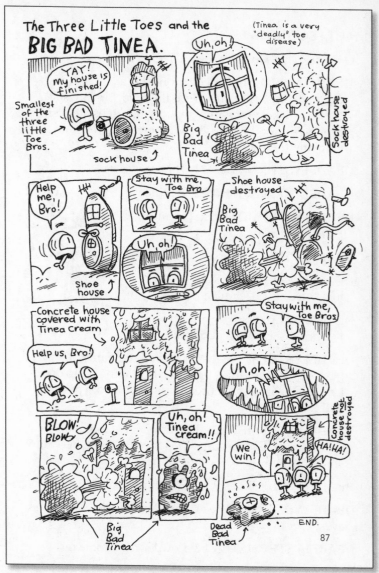

Terry's version of 'The Three Little Pigs and the Big Bad Wolf' from *What Body Part is That?*

ACT I SCENE ONE

On a dusty windowsill, somewhere in any house.

DEADFLYELLA: [using her proboscis as a vacuum cleaner] Alas, poor me. Here I am working myself to the exoskeleton while my horrible stepsisters sit around on their fat little abdomens laughing and enjoying themselves.

DEADFLYSTEPSISTER #1: Ha ha!

DEADFLYSTEPSISTER #2: Hee hee!

DEADFLYSTEPMOTHER: [vomiting] BLEUGH! BLEUGH!

DEADFLYELLA: Oh gross, deadfly puke!

DEADFLYSTEPSISTER #1: Well don't just stare at it, Deadflyella. Eat it up!

DEADFLYELLA: [sucking it up with her proboscis] Alas, poor me.

DEADFLYSTEPSISTER #2: Oh well, we can't sit around here all day watching Deadflyella making a pig of herself. We have to get ready for the Deadflyprince's ball.

DEADFLYSTEPSISTER #1: Yes, we have to make ourselves really beautiful. Deadflyella, come here and shine my wings.

DEADFLYSTEPSISTER #2: Brush my bristles!

DEADFLYSTEPSISTER #1: Polish my large compound eyes!

DEADFLYSTEPSISTER #2: Powder my proboscis!

'Deadflyella' is a play based on the story of Cinderella, but with a cast made up of dead flies (*Just Disgusting!*).

Mud Brown and the Seven Slobs

Once upon a slime there was a disgusting princess called Mud Brown. She lived in a stinking bog with seven slobs called Stinky, Filthy, Snotty, Messy, Grubby, Sloppy and Robert.

Mud Brown and the seven slobs ate dirt, put mud in their underpants, sneezed in each other's faces, shoved handfuls of worms in their ears and never EVER brushed their teeth.

One day an unhandsome prince called Prince Poopy-pants came riding through the forest on a filthy wart-hog and saw Mud Brown and the seven slobs having a wild mud fight.

Prince Poopy-pants looked at Mud Brown's filthy clothes, dirty face, matted hair and ears full of nasty wriggling worms, and fell in love with her at once.

He leapt from his wart-hog and waded into the bog towards her. 'You are the dirtiest, most perfectly despicable princess I have ever laid my beady, bloodshot eyes on!' he said. 'Will you marry me?'

Mud Brown scooped up a big handful of mud and slammed it right in the prince's face. 'Of course I will,' she said. 'I've been waiting all my life for someone as unhandsome, unappealing and unhygienic as you!'

Prince Poopy-pants and Mud Brown embraced and kissed but, unfortunately, as neither of them had ever cleaned their teeth in their entire lives, the combined stench of their terrible breath formed a cloud so toxic that it not only killed them both, but also Stinky, Filthy, Snotty, Messy, Grubby, Sloppy and Robert. And nobody lived ever after.

THE END

My disgusting version of 'Snow White and the Seven Dwarfs' (*The Very Bad Book*).

TRY THIS

Once upon a slime …

Choose a fairy tale and write your own 'slimy' version of it. If you like you can choose two fairy tales and combine them. Alternatively, you could mix and match lots of different elements and characters from a range of fairy tales to create your own original super-slimy fairy tale.

Slimy fairy-tale titles

- Little Green Snotting Hood
- The Three Little Idiots and the Big Bad Moron
- Cindersmeller
- Blood Red and the Seven Little Vampires
- Sleeping Ugly
- Snoring Beauty
- The Bog Prince
- The Princess and the Pee
- The Princess and the Poo
- The Little DUH! maid

30. Pets and other animals

I used to have a dog called Sooty. When he wasn't fighting the other dogs in the street or trying to get the female dogs in the neighbourhood pregnant, he was chasing cars and attempting to bite their tyres. He never gave up ... not even after he was hit by a car.

He just got back up, coughed a bit of blood, ran home, went into his kennel and slept for a whole weekend. And then on Monday, yep, you guessed it, he was out on the street again chasing cars.

I always admired Sooty's full-on, joyful approach to life and especially his determination, which is I guess why he appears in so many of the Just stories ('Playing dead', 'The dog ate it', 'Cake of doom', 'Mudmen', etc.).

The real Sooty in an uncharacteristically peaceful moment.

Actually, come to think of it, dogs appear in lots of my other books, too.

The bad dog from *The Very Bad Book*, the dog on a cog from *The Cat on the Mat is Flat* and Barky the Barking Dog from *The 13-Storey Treehouse*.

Other pets I've owned over the years are tortoises (kind of sad), axolotls (kind of boring), tadpoles (kind of 'just to feed the axolotls' but actually more entertaining than axolotls), tropical fish (kind of expensive), cats (kind of scratchy) and, of course, sea-monkeys.

As a child I was intrigued by the ads for sea-monkeys, which made them look like semi-human creatures that lived in elaborate underwater kingdoms, so I saved up and bought some sea-monkey eggs. I added the water and waited for the magical creatures to materialise. The sea-monkeys came to life, all right, but they were not the exciting pets I was hoping for. After all, they are just brine shrimp—a type of minuscule wriggly bug.

In *The 13-Storey Treehouse,* Terry's sea-monkey eggs hatch into *actual* monkeys!

There are lots of animals in the Treehouse books. The character Jill lives with thirteen flying cats, two dogs, a goat, three horses, four goldfish, one cow, six rabbits, two guinea pigs, one camel and one donkey ...

but Silky is definitely her favourite.

Andy and Terry also have animals in the treehouse including ice-skating penguins and man-eating sharks.

The 13-Storey Treehouse

Ice-skating penguins from *The 26-Storey Treehouse.*

TRY THIS

50-word pet story

Tell a story about—or describe—a pet you own or have owned (or would LIKE to own) in exactly 50 words. See how much of your pet's personality you can convey in those 50 precious words.

It may help to write the story first and then subtract any words that aren't strictly essential until you have 50. Your title can be any length.

31. Pocket books

Long before I was an 'officially published' writer, I used to produce my own 12-page pocket books. Some of my most popular titles were a practical-joking guide called *Just Tricking!*, a self-help book called *How to Stop Yourself from Becoming a Slug* and an action-thriller called *The Day My Bum Went Psycho*.

I used to sell these little books at markets and bookshops around Melbourne for $1 each. On a good day I could make around $30 to $40, but the real reward was that I started getting feedback on my writing—both positive and negative—which helped me to improve much faster than I might have done otherwise.

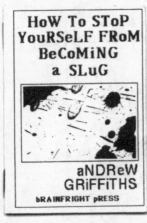

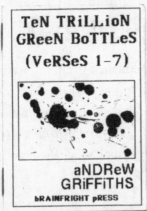

Some of my self-published pocket books.

Pocket books are a great way to present your writing to other people ... and they're really easy to make! All you need is an A4 sheet of paper, a pair of scissors and a stapler, and you're ready to go.

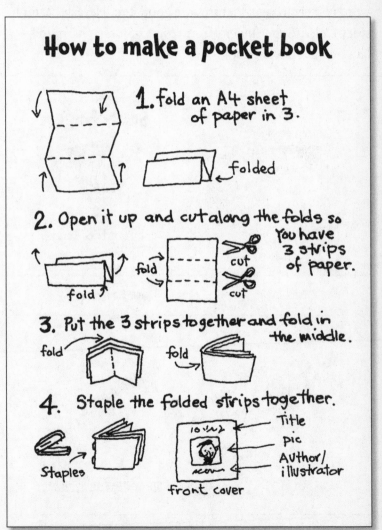

How to make a pocket book

1. Fold an A4 sheet of paper in 3.

folded

2. Open it up and cut along the folds so you have 3 strips of paper.

fold   fold   cut
fold   cut

3. Put the 3 strips together and fold in the middle.

fold   fold

4. Staple the folded strips together.

Staples

Title
pic
Author/illustrator
front cover

I always like to start by designing a front cover. The process of writing my name, drawing a picture and thinking up a fun title to match helps to get me in the mood. Pocket books are also fun to write because you only have to write a few words on each page. Pictures are good, too. Here's a cartoon story called 'Superfinger' (from *The 13-Storey Treehouse*) laid out as a pocket book.

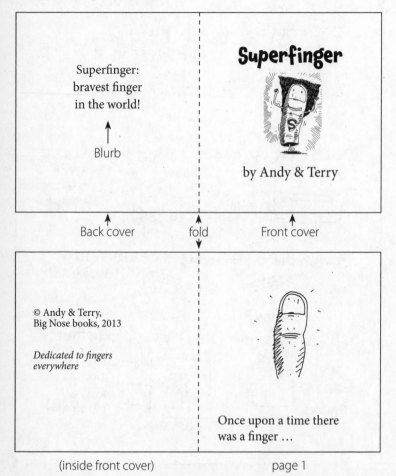

But it was no ordinary finger ... it was a super finger!

One day Superfinger was out looking for problems requiring finger-based solutions when he heard a rock concert.

Flying in for a closer look, Superfinger could see that onstage was his favourite guitarist, Jimi Handrix.

But as he watched, Superfinger saw that Jimi was in trouble. He'd started a guitar solo that was so epic he didn't have enough fingers to play it!

This looks like a job for Superfinger!!

page 6

Superfinger flew onto the stage and launched himself headfirst at the fretboard of Jimi's guitar.

page 7

The crowd went wild!

page 8

Superfinger and Jimi jammed for the rest of the night and everybody agreed it was the best concert ever in the history of the entire world.

page 9
(inside back cover)

TRY THIS

Make a pocket book

Making a pocket book is one of my favourite writing-workshop activities and it seems to work for writers of all ages and abilities. Fold an A4 sheet of paper into three strips. Cut along the folds. Fold these pieces and staple (see diagram on page 225).

If you want to make a larger book with fewer pages, cut an A4 sheet of paper into two strips (not three). This will give you an eight-page book with more space on each page for words and pictures.

One of the best things about pocket books is that your writing can be in any form you like. It can be a story, a list, an instruction manual, an illustrated guide, a recount, etc. Almost all of the writing activities in this book could be presented in the form of a pocket book.

Use some of the story titles below to help get you started:

- 9 ways to annoy your brother/sister
- 9 things you should know about (insert your favourite place/subject/activity here)
- 9 things I HATE!
- 9 things I LOVE!
- How to have fun in (insert the name of the place you live here)
- How to play football

- How to cheat at Monopoly
- The day I ...
- The day my cat went shopping
- Super-ninja granny
- The day my sister put a cotton bud up her nose
- 9 terrifying facts about turtles
- How to kill a bug
- The tomato monster
- How to be a REAL man
- How to be a REAL woman

Use the Random idea generator on pages 336–7 to help you come up with other titles.

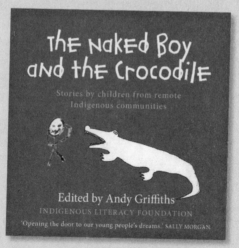

The Naked Boy and the Crocodile is a collection of pocket books made by children in remote Indigenous communities. (You can order copies from www.indigenousliteracyfoundation.org.au)

Here is a man
called Three-coat Keith.
He wears one coat on top
and two underneath.

32. Poems

It's probably pretty obvious that I like writing poems: I've done two whole books full of them (*The Cat on the Mat is Flat* and *The Big Fat Cow That Goes Kapow*), plus there are lots of poems in *The Bad Book* and *The Very Bad Book*, and I even managed to put some in the Just books and the Treehouse books.

I used the 'John and Betty'-style early readers that I learned to read with as the basis for a 25-verse poem. (The 'John and Betty' readers were not as action-packed as my poem, however!)

Learn to read with Andy

See me jump.

See me run.

See me hop.

It is fun.

See me hop.

See me run.

See me jump.

Fun, fun, fun.

See me jump.

On my bed.

I jump so high

I bump my head.

On the ceiling.

On the roof.

I hit it hard.

Ouch! Ugh! Oof!

The first two verses of 'Learn to read with Andy' (from *Just Crazy!*).

'The cat, the mat, the rat, and the baseball bat' is one of the most popular rhymes in *The Cat on the Mat is Flat*.

The cat sat.
The cat sat on the mat.
The cat sat on the mat
and as it sat it saw a rat.

The cat jumped up
and chased the rat
around and around
and around the mat.

The rat did not like
being chased by the cat,
and after three laps
around the mat
the rat said,
'That's enough of that!'
And it went and got ...

a baseball bat.

The rat chased the cat.
The rat chased the cat
with the baseball bat.
Around and around
and around the mat
the rat chased the cat
with the baseball bat
until ...

KERSPLAT!

Never again did that cat
chase the rat—
the cat was much too flat for that.

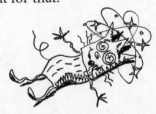

The Cat on the Mat is Flat

Ten unlucky pirates
swinging on a vine ...
One fell off
and then there were nine.

Eeeee-yaahhhhhhhhh!

GO TO BED!

I'm lying on the couch
reading a book[1]
when Mum comes in
and gives me THAT look.[2]

'Andy?' she says.
'Did you hear what I said?
Put down that book
and GO TO BED!'[3]

But there's no way
I'm going to bed.[4]
It's time to stall.
It's time to beg.

[1] It's really cool. It's about this kid who won't go to bed.
[2] You know the one.
[3] I did hear, but I'm pretending I didn't.
[4] I bet Action Man doesn't go to bed at 8.30.

The poem 'Ten unlucky pirates' appears in *The 26-Storey Treehouse*.

'Go to bed!' is a story told completely in verse in *Just Disgusting!*

Ruth and her incredibly annoying hooter are from *The Big Fat Cow That Goes Kapow*.

Here comes Ruth.
Ruth rides a scooter.
Ruth rides a scooter
with a super-loud hooter.

The terrifying Mermaidia reveals her plans for Terry in *The 13-Storey Treehouse*.

Little Willy
Little Willy took a match
And set fire to his bum.
Said Little Willy as it burnt,
'Gee, that was pretty dumb.'

Little Willy from *The Bad Book*.

TRY THIS

Write a rhyming poem

Try doing a single-sound poem like the ones in *The Cat on the Mat is Flat* and *The Big Fat Cow That Goes Kapow*. Choose a word sound (e.g. 'un') and then write down as many words that you can think of that have that sound (e.g. bun, begun, done, fun, gun, nun, none, pun, run, sun, shun, spun, stun, ton, won). Then look over your list for ideas of how these words could be used together to tell a story.

There was a duck.
His name was Chuck.
Chuck the Duck
drove an ice-cream truck.

But one wet day Chuck's truck got stuck.

'What bad luck,'
said Chuck the Duck.
'My ice-cream truck
is stuck in muck.'

The Cat on the Mat is Flat

Note: Online rhyming dictionaries are a great source of rhyming words.

... OR THIS

Poetic parody

Base a poem on a poem (or a song) that you already know.

There was
an old lady
who swallowed a poo.
I don't know why she
    swallowed that poo,
Perhaps
she'll spew.

This is based on 'The Old Lady Who Swallowed a Fly'.

Humpty Dumpty spray-painted the wall
He covered it with his offensive scrawl.
All the King's horses and all the King's men
Confiscated his spray-can
    and smashed his head in.

This is based on the nursery rhyme 'Humpty Dumpty'.

238

33. Posters & signs

If you want to get people's attention and provide them with information (and you can't afford to hire a sky-writing plane or rent billboard space), I can think of no better way to get your message across than a poster or a sign.

They are also a great storytelling device, and my books are full of them.

Just Doomed!

Just Doomed!

Just Macbeth!

Just Macbeth!

Just Stupid!

*The Big Fat Cow
That Goes Kapow*

The 26-Storey Treehouse

The 13-Storey Treehouse

One day while out walking
by the sea,
I saw a sign saying,
'BEWARE OF THE BEE.
YOU'LL GET STUNG
UNLESS YOU FLEE!'

The Cat on the Mat is Flat

The 26-Storey Treehouse

The Very Bad Book

The Cat on the Mat is Flat

The 13-Storey Treehouse

When Silky goes missing in *The 13-Storey Treehouse*, Jill makes a poster.

In the story 'A really, really good excuse', Andy discovers he is wanted by the police when he comes across this poster.

Just Shocking!

Posters can also advertise cool new services and products ... whether they exist or not!

BRAIN-A-RAMA

DISCOUNT

BRAIN SURGERY & STEAM CLEANING

Having trouble remembering?
Can't think things through clearly?
Always doing dumb things?
Why not let Brain-a-rama recharge
and steam clean your brain?
$25 per hemisphere
$40 for whole brain
$500 total mind massage
$2000 complete brain cell boost

SPECIAL
OFFER—
this month
only

50-DOG BREAD

Guaranteed no less than
50 dogs in every loaf!

THE AMAZING SPOONCIL!

It's not a spoon
and it's not a pencil ...
IT'S BOTH!!!

TRY THIS

Design a poster

Make an eye-catching poster for an imaginary product, service, band, movie, book, gadget, food, holiday destination, or anything else you would like to advertise.

Effective posters are ones in which the main bit of information can be gleaned at a glance—don't include too much information.

Suggestions for posters:

- Wanted (new parents, new brain, new brother or sister, etc.)
- An incredible new food (e.g. flying monkey-flavoured ice-cream)
- An imaginary movie (e.g. *Killer Koalas from Outer Space, Brando the Nasty Rubber Ducky*)
- A fantastic holiday destination (perhaps on Mars, Mount Everest or the bottom of the ocean)
- A band or concert
- A great new gadget (let your imagination run wild)
- A warning poster (e.g. slippery when slippery, beware invisible cows)

34. Quizzes & tests

I REALLY like tests and quizzes—both doing them and making them up. I have used tests instead of blurbs on the back covers of all the Just books.

You may notice, of course, that no matter what score you get on these tests, the answers indicate that you will love the book—but hey, I never said these were proper tests ... they're back-cover blurbs, which are designed to encourage you to read the book!

Is this the right book for you?
Take the crazy test and find out.

YES NO

☐ ☐ Do you bounce so high on your bed that you hit your head on the ceiling?

☐ ☐ Do you ever look in the mirror and see a crazy maniac staring back at you?

☐ ☐ Do you like to read stories about kittens, puppies and ponies getting mashed and pulverised?

☐ ☐ Do you sometimes get the urge to take your clothes off and cover yourself in mud?

☐ ☐ Do you often waste your time taking crazy tests like this one?

SCORE: One point for each 'yes' answer.

3–5   You are completely crazy. You will love this book.

1–2   You are not completely crazy, but you're not far off it. You will love this book.

0   You are so crazy you don't even realise you're crazy. You will love this book.

Just Crazy! back cover blurb

246

Terry likes creating quizzes too, as you can see from these examples.

① MORAY EEL ② BIRD ③ SNAKE
④ SHARK ⑤ TOAD ⑥ RHINO
⑦ HIPPO ⑧ SPIDER ⑨ MONKEY
⑩ FISH ⑪ BULLDOG ⑫ SNAIL

If you had to kiss one of the above pairs of lips, which pair would you choose?

What Body Part is That?

What Body Part is That?

In 'Would you rather?' in *Just Annoying!*, Andy spends the whole story testing his family's patience by quizzing them about whether they'd rather be eaten by ants or lions or rather be squashed by bricks or feathers.

Just Annoying!

You can create quizzes for almost anything you can think of. Here is one I wrote to help people decide whether or not they are a cardboard box. Confused? Take the quiz!

Are you a cardboard box?

Take the CARDBOARD BOX test and find out!

YES NO

☐ ☐ After you have a shower do you end up all soggy and stuck to the tiles?

☐ ☐ When you're having breakfast do people pick you up by the neck and try to shake cornflakes out of your mouth into their bowls?

☐ ☐ When you're trying to walk down the street does the wind just blow you along with all the other bits of rubbish?

☐ ☐ When you travel on trains does the conductor insist that you ride in the freight car with the rest of the packages?

☐ ☐ Do you have trouble making telephone calls because you have no ears, mouth or fingers?

Score: One point for each 'yes' answer.

3–5   You are a cardboard box.

1–2   You have a lot in common with cardboard boxes.

0   You are not a cardboard box.

How to tell if you are a CHICKEN

Do you have feathers?

Are your legs like drumsticks?

They even smell like chicken.

Have you ever found yourself in a hot oven surrounded by hot potatoes?

Mum! Dad!

If your answer to any of these questions is YES, then you are a chicken.

249

TRY THIS

Create a quiz

1. Do you like creating crazy questions?
2. Do you like asking people to make choices?
3. Do you like thinking up things for people to make decisions about?
4. Do you like coming up with questions and a variety of answers?
5. Do you like quizzes?

If you answered 'yes' to any of the above questions then you will definitely enjoy creating your own quiz!

It could be a multiple-choice quiz where you give the quizee several answers to choose from, or just a straight yes or no quiz.

Your quiz can be as silly or as sensible as you like.

Don't forget to include a scoring system!

A great way to get started is to brainstorm at least 20 possible quiz titles. I'm sure at least one will inspire you.

Just Macbeth!

35. Rules (and how to break them)

I love writing stories about characters who break rules. In fact, pretty much *all* of my stories are about some form of rule breaking. Whether the rules being broken are school rules, road rules, rules to do with good manners and polite behaviour, or simply the conventions of storytelling, my characters are all out there breaking as many as they can.

The Very Bad Book

'Bad Terence' from *The Bad Book*

'Penny McRose' from *The Bad Book*

The Very Bad Book

MR SHUSH'S TOP 10 LIST OF THINGS YOU SHOULD NEVER DO TO A BOOK

1. Attach two ropes to a book and attach one end of each rope to a horse and then move the horses away from each other until the rope tightens and the book is ripped apart.

2. Pulverise a book into atoms, pulverise the atoms into quarks, and then pulverise the quarks into even smaller particles that are so tiny they haven't even got a name.

3. Lick all the print off a book, no matter how good it tastes.

4. Put a book in a fish tank, even if it's a book about fish.

5. Tear the pages of a book into tiny little bits and throw them in the air to make a snow storm.

6. Use the pages of a book to make origami animals.

7. Attach wheels to a book and use it as a skateboard.

8. Use a book as a shield while having a sword fight.

9. Use a book as a hat on a rainy day.

10. Put a book in a rocket and send it into space (zero gravity is very bad for books—it makes all the words float up off the page).

Robot Riot!

In 'Expel me', Andy comes back to school after the holidays and tries to break every rule he can think of in order to get expelled so that he doesn't have to go to school any more.

*i*t's the first day back at school.

And if all goes to plan it will also be my last.

I'm sitting up the back corner of the classroom. Well, I'm not really sitting. I'm leaning back on the chair, putting all my weight on the back legs, just like we're not supposed to.

And that's not the only rule I'm breaking.

My feet are up on the desk. I'm not wearing any shoes. I'm wearing a cap. My T-shirt is ripped. Plus it has a rude slogan on the front. I've got my Walkman on. On the table in front of me is a packet of bubblegum, a spitball shooter and some freshly chewed spitballs. On the blackboard I've drawn this crazy-looking stick figure with bugged-out eyes and buck teeth. It's hitting itself over the head with a hammer and saying 'Look at me—I'm your stupid new teacher!' And underneath it I've written 'By Andy Griffiths' so that there's no chance anybody else will get the blame.

> I figure the new teacher will be like all new teachers. They'll be wanting to show everybody how tough they are. They won't be wanting to muck around with warnings or detentions or phone calls to parents. They'll be looking for a scapegoat to send straight to the principal's office. Well, they won't have to look for long. Here I am—ready and willing.

Just Stupid!

Unfortunately, Andy's new teacher has a very different approach to classroom discipline from any other teacher Andy has ever had, and he finds that she refuses to accept that he's done anything wrong.

In real life, however, it's pretty easy to get into trouble for breaking rules. Because, when you think about it, there are just so many.

Just Stupid!

TRY THIS

Write a list of rules

Make a list of all the rules you have been taught throughout your life. Just write them down as they come to mind. See if you can come up with 10. If you get to 10, go for 20. Use the following list to get you started.

- School rules (homework, uniform)
- Parental rules (bedtime, chores)
- Safety rules (road safety, water safety, home safety, etc.)
- Hygiene rules (wash your hands after going to the bathroom, cover your mouth when you cough)
- Etiquette (say please and thank you, don't speak with your mouth full)
- Silly rules (don't make faces because if the wind changes you'll be stuck like that forever, don't feed dynamite to your dog)

... OR THIS

Break a rule

Choose one of the rules from your list that you would really like to break. Now write about yourself actually breaking that rule. When I do this, I like to write in first-person present tense:

I am sitting in the classroom. I take off my shirt. I take off my pants. I am completely nude ...

36. Scripts

Sometimes I begin stories just by writing a conversation between two characters and seeing where it leads. These are not necessarily scripts to be performed—they are just a useful way of exploring characters and ideas without all the bother of plot and story (although strangely enough, these often emerge out of the conversations).

'Fun with a fire hose', the first story in *Just Shocking!*, is based on a conversation that I had with my daughter (when she was four) while watching some people having a picnic. I thought it sounded exactly like the sort of thing that Andy and Danny might talk about when they're between stories ...

DANNY: Hey, Andy, I've been thinking, and you know what? I reckon we could have a lot of fun with a fire hose.

ANDY: A fire hose?

DANNY: Yeah! See those people in that park having a picnic?

ANDY: Yes, I see them, but what have they got to do with a fire hose?

DANNY: Well, if we had a fire hose, we could point it at them, turn it on and they would all go flying everywhere!

ANDY: Great idea, Danny!

DANNY: Thanks.

ANDY: Just one question.

DANNY: What's that?

ANDY: Why would we want to do that?

DANNY: For FUN, of course! Just imagine it! All those drenched people rolling around in the wet grass, waving their arms and yelling, 'Help! Help!', and trying to stand up! And you know what we would do then?

ANDY: What?

DANNY: We would just turn the hose up even harder and blast them all back down again!

ANDY: That doesn't sound like much fun for them.

DANNY: Well, no, but it would be fun for us. And don't forget—the pressure from the hose would be so strong it would blast everybody's clothes off ...

Just Shocking!

Scripts don't only have to be about humans. Anything can have a conversation with anything else ... For instance, 'Deadflyella' in *Just Disgusting!* is a play based on the story of Cinderella, but with a cast made up of dead flies.

Or, as Terry has shown in the Just books, even page numbers can become characters capable of having dramatic conversations ...

Just Doomed!

Just Macbeth! is a Just book in which the characters from the Just series get tangled up in the Shakespearean play *Macbeth*. In the following scene, Lisa (who thinks she is Lady Macbeth) tries to convince Andy (who thinks he is Macbeth) to kill King Duncan so they can become King and Queen.

LISA: If we're going to be King and Queen, Duncan has to go.

ANDY: You don't mean ...

LISA: Yes.

ANDY: *Murder him?*

LISA: Yes.

ANDY: But why?

LISA: Because as long as he lives, you can't be King! Which means that I can't be Queen.

ANDY: But, murdering Duncan? That would be ... well ... murder!

LISA: Well ... I suppose that's *one* way of looking at it.

ANDY: But we can't.

LISA: Why not?

ANDY: Well, we don't have a good reason for a start.

LISA: Yes we do.

ANDY: No we don't.

LISA: Do you want to be King?

ANDY: Yes, but ...

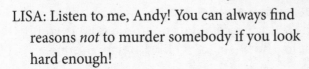

LISA: Listen to me, Andy! You can always find reasons *not* to murder somebody if you look hard enough!

ANDY: Yes, but there's no need to *murder* him: he might die of natural causes.

LISA: Maybe you're right. Maybe you *will* become King without killing Duncan—but it might not be for a *really* long time. By the time it happens, you'll be too old to enjoy being King. You'll have all the Wizz Fizz you ever wanted and you'll be like, 'Oh ... I'm so old ... I can hardly eat one teaspoon of Wizz Fizz without choking to death.' Is that what you want, Andy?

ANDY: N-no ...

LISA: Then it's settled! You can either die a horrible painful needless death choking on Wizz Fizz ... or you can simply kill the King. Not exactly a hard decision, is it?

ANDY: [*frowning*] No ... I suppose not.

Just Macbeth!

TRY THIS

Write a script

Write a short conversation in script form for one of the following situations. You don't have to write a whole story; just have fun writing the conversation and see where it leads. If you are happy with the results, you and a friend could use it as the basis for a short performance.

- A dog trying to convince his owner to increase his pocket money
- Two goldfish daring each other to jump out of the bowl
- A monkey trying to convince a zookeeper that he is in fact not a monkey and should be released
- Two dinosaurs arguing about what is the best prehistoric television show
- An apple and a banana trying to convince a person to eat them first
- A bum and a head having an argument about who is the more important body part
- Two kids arguing about who has the tougher dad
- Two dads arguing about who has the tougher kid

... OR THIS

Answer the question

You are faced with a very angry parent who has just asked you one of the questions below. Choose one and write down the conversation that follows.

- Why is your sister crying?
- Why isn't the dog breathing?
- How did the goldfish get in the toaster?
- How did a tractor get on the roof?

37. Snapshots

One of the things I like to do in the early stages of writing a story is to draw what I call 'snapshots' or 'frozen moments' of scenes from the story. I imagine that the characters have a photo album that contains pictures of certain scenes from their lives. Here are some 'snapshots' I did while working on *The 13-Storey Treehouse*. They are very rough first drafts in which I am just trying to get potential story ideas down as quickly as possible.

Snapshots from the Treehouse photo album

Terry chases Andy all around the treehouse with a giant Banana

A + T hit golf balls from the Treehouse turret

~~Two girls~~ The Marshmallow machine is malfunctioning

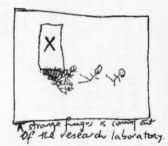

A strange fungus is coming out of the research laboratory.

~~Terry~~ giving medicine to one of the sick sharks in the Shark tank

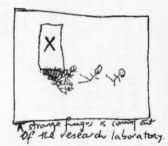

Terry forgets to put the LID on the popcorn ~~machine~~ pot (Again.)

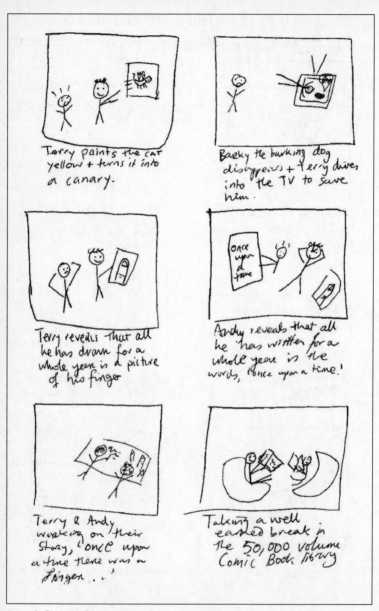

Rough first-draft snapshots from my notebook.

I didn't use all these ideas in the final book and many were changed as I wrote the story, but the process of drawing and labelling the snapshots helped me picture the world of the treehouse and get to know the types of things that were going to happen there. Here are some of my snapshots that made it into the finished book (redrawn by Terry of course!).

Terry paints the cat yellow and turns it into a canary.

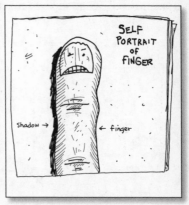

Terry reveals that all he has drawn for a whole year is a picture of his finger.

Terry hits Andy with a giant banana.

Terry and Andy working on their story 'Once upon a time there was a finger ...'.

Another great thing about snapshots is that as well as helping to picture scenes within your story, you can use them to create dramatic openings.

Many of the short stories in the Just books begin with a clearly defined moment. For instance, 'Bogeyboy' begins with the image of Andy lying under his sister's bed waiting to scare her because she teased him about wetting the bed.

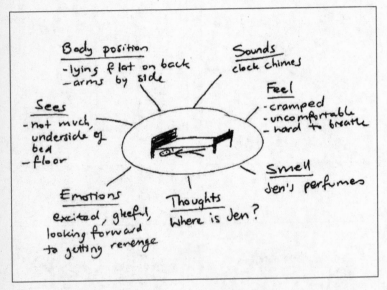

The snapshot with a few notes.

Once I have a strong image for the beginning of a story, I like to sketch it and then spend some time thinking about all the things my character might be feeling, hearing, seeing, etc., as in the example above.

I then take all this information and try to write a focused beginning that includes as many of these details as I think the reader needs in order to be drawn into the story.

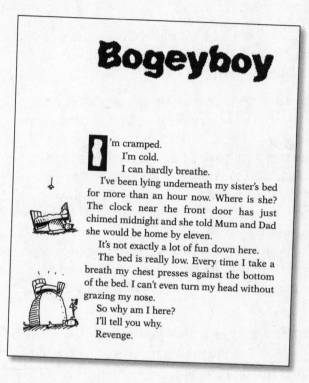

Bogeyboy

I'm cramped.
I'm cold.
I can hardly breathe.

I've been lying underneath my sister's bed for more than an hour now. Where is she? The clock near the front door has just chimed midnight and she told Mum and Dad she would be home by eleven.

It's not exactly a lot of fun down here.

The bed is really low. Every time I take a breath my chest presses against the bottom of the bed. I can't even turn my head without grazing my nose.

So why am I here?

I'll tell you why.

Revenge.

The opening scene of 'Bogeyboy' in *Just Stupid!*

I like to start my stories this way because it plunges the reader right into the middle of the scene. Having established where the character is, what they're doing and how they're feeling, I then fill the reader in on whatever else they need to know before the action of the story begins for real.

TRY THIS

Snapshot

This is a three-part exercise designed to help you take a specific moment from your life and explore the rich sensory detail that all such moments contain.

1. Pretend you have an imaginary camera that is able to take a photograph of a moment from your life that sticks in your mind for some reason. It could be a time you got into trouble, a time you were scared, a time you were embarrassed, amused, sad, happy or simply content. Often the moment just before a significant event can be a good one to choose. Draw a sketch of your imaginary photograph (stick figures are fine!). Note: You are just drawing a single moment, not a sequence of events.

2. Label your snapshot like the example shown on page 273. Write at least three details under each of the headings.

See: What visual details stick in your mind?

Hear: What sounds were happening around you?

Feel: Were you holding anything in your hands? Were they clenched? Open?

Smell/taste: Is there any specific smell or taste associated with your memory?

Body position: What was your body doing? Where were your arms? Your legs?

Thoughts: What was your main thought at that exact moment?

Emotions/feelings: What was your main emotion or feeling at that moment?

Dialogue: Were you saying something to yourself? To somebody else? Was somebody saying something to you?

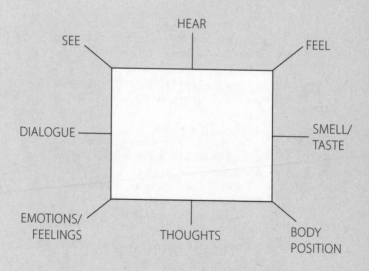

3. Now is the fun part where you get to convert your snapshot into words. I either like to start with the words 'I am ...' or with a line of dialogue. When you've done this, and perhaps tested it out by reading it to somebody else, you will have a solid starting point for telling either a true, partially true or completely made-up story.

ou know when you have one of those perfect moments where everything is just ... you know ... *perfect*?

Well I'm having one right now.

The sun is shining, the birds are singing, the breeze is blowing and my hair is looking great.

But wait, there's more!

I've also got a double-scoop ice-cream with sprinkles and chocolate flakes and I'm just about to take my first lick.

I wish this moment could last forever.

But, of course, it can't.

The sun is too hot and the ice-cream is already too soft for that.

I have to take my first lick soon or there'll be nothing left.

Andy enjoying a perfect moment at the start of the story 'Lick' (*Just Doomed!*).

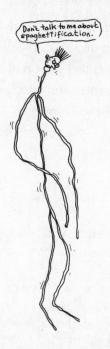

38. Stretching the truth

Readers often ask me if the stories in the Just books are true. The truth is that they are sort of true and sort of not true. A lot of the stories in this series are based on things that really happened to me or to someone I know, but in the process of turning them into fiction, I often have to stretch the truth in order to make them funnier and/or more entertaining.

'Busting!' (*Just Stupid!*)

This story, which culminates in Andy putting out a burning shopping centre with only his … well … you know, has a number of true elements. I once had trouble finding a toilet in a large shopping centre and another time I had a dream that I was going to the toilet only to wake up and find that I actually was, but these two events were not linked in the way they are in the story.

Suddenly I know what I have to do. I can solve my problem and be a hero at the same time.

'Excuse me,' I say, 'you're not going to need those back-up units.'

'What are you talking about?' he says.

'You've got me,' I say.

'Huh?'

'Watch this!' I say.

I go as close to the burning building as I can. I grab hold of my fly. I take aim.

Ahhhhhhhhhhhhhhhhh. Relief! Beautiful relief. The fire is powerless against me. It disappears in clouds of steam. People are gathered around applauding. The supermarket manager is there. And the pencil seller. And the hippie. Even the old man. Cheering.

Just Stupid!

'In the shower with Andy' (*Just Annoying!*)

In this story, Andy completely fills a shower cubicle with water by sealing it up with silicone glue. In real life I've tried many times to fill the shower cubicle with water by putting the face washer over the plughole and standing on it, but I would never be brave—or silly—enough to go as far as Andy does in his quest for shower-cubicle glory.

I stretch the truth to make the story more interesting and more fun. To begin this process I take a real incident and then ask *what's the worst thing that could happen next?* I then keep telling the story as if that worst thing really *did* happen and how, in the process of trying to fix it, another even worse thing happened ... and then another ... and another until I reach a point at which things seemingly can't possibly get any worse ... and then they do. (Yes, it takes a lot of brainstorming and patience and time ... but it's worth it!)

'Gorillagram' (*Just Tricking!*)

I once dressed up in a gorilla costume and embarrassed my sister at her birthday party in a restaurant, but it's not true that I couldn't get the zipper undone afterwards and nobody called the zookeepers.

'Murder, bloody murder!' (*Just Annoying!*)

My cousin, David, and I used to yell out stupid things in the backyard, such as 'Murder, bloody murder!', in an attempt to get the neighbour's attention. And I *did* have a neighbour called Mr Broadbent, but he never got so annoyed that he actually tried to murder me.

Part of the art of stretching the truth, of course, is to do it in a way that keeps your reader believing your story. Anchoring your story with real-life events and using lots of small realistic details all help to add an air of authenticity to your storytelling. Another important technique is to use a no-nonsense, matter-of-fact tone of voice as if the crazy stuff you are writing about actually happened and is the most normal thing in the world. For instance, it was a lot of fun making up 'body part facts' for *What Body Part is That?* The facts, of course, are ridiculous but stated so seriously and reasonably that we almost believe them, against our better judgement.

A&T'S FUN BODY PART FACT #2

In ancient times people used to grow their hair really long and wrap it around their bodies because clothes hadn't been invented yet.

A&T'S FUN BODY PART FACT #3

Every year in Australia more than 300 people have their faces ripped off by killer koalas from outer space.

A&T'S FUN BODY PART FACT #6

When you go up to a high elevation, your ears pop. If you go up too high, however, your whole head will explode.

What Body Part is That?

In '101 really dangerous things', Andy attempts to pass off many completely ridiculous 'facts' as completely true and it's often this tension between his certainty and the nonsensical nature of what he's saying that makes us laugh.

31. Girl germs. (Shocking fact #1: Girl germs have been scientifically proven—by me and my best friend, Danny—to be the most dangerous germs on the planet. Anybody who has ever TOUCHED a girl, been in the SAME ROOM as a girl or even THOUGHT about a girl should immediately run to the nearest hospital before it is too late. Anybody who IS a girl, well, bad luck. It already IS too late. You are doomed.)

Just Shocking!

TRY THIS

What's the worst thing that could happen next?

Spend some time considering the worst thing that could happen next in each of the following situations. Choose one and write down at least five possible worst-case scenarios. Pick the scenario that most interests you and, using the 'what's the worst thing that could happen next?' technique, see if you can create the outline for a short story.

1. You see a ten-dollar note lying on the footpath and bend down to pick it up

2. Your parents have told you a thousand times not to throw balls in the house but you do anyway

3. You accidentally swallow a fly

4. A giant fly accidentally swallows you

5. You are at the show and your friend dares you to take a ride on 'The tower of terror' and declares that you are an absolute chicken if you don't

... OR THIS

Make the unbelievable believable

Add a made-up piece of nonsense to the end of each of the following sentence beginnings.

- Scientific studies show ...
- I heard on the news that ...
- Recent research findings prove that ...
- Statistics show ...
- Experts say ...
- It's a well-known fact that ...
- Nine out of ten doctors recommend ...

Scientists testing the truth of the nursery rhyme 'Rock-a-bye baby' in *The 26-Storey Treehouse*.

THIS LOOKS LIKE A JOB FOR SUPERFINGER!!

39. Superblank!

I like creating unusual superheroes and super-villains.

Superfinger (from *The 13-Storey Treehouse*) is a superhero who solves problems requiring finger-based solutions, such as pointing the way for lost people, helping to clear blocked noses and holding strings so people can tie parcels.

The 13-Storey Treehouse

Here are some other superheroes who use their body parts or body-part-related products for good (from *What Body Part is That?*).

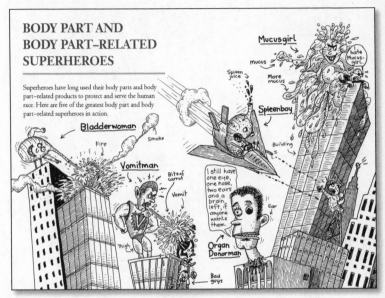

What Body Part is That?

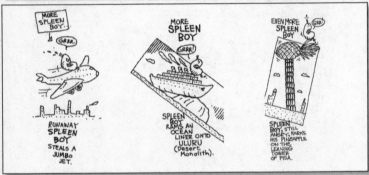

Just Shocking!

Sooty the Wonder Dog, on the other hand, doesn't really live up to his name—he doesn't seem to do anything that wonderful.

Just Disgusting!   *Just Crazy!*

In *The Day My Bum Went Psycho*, Zack Freeman calls a bum-catcher when his bum detaches itself from his body and runs away. He quickly finds himself drawn into a world of super bum-fighting heroes and meets such legends as Silas Sterne, The Kicker, The Smacker and The Kisser. To Zack's complete surprise he discovers that he has previously unrealised bum-fighting powers.

The legendary bum-fighters, the B-Team from *The Day My Bum Went Psycho*.

The greatest super-villain Terry and I have ever created, however, would have to be Super Bad Bird!

Unless, of course, you count Super Bad Squirrel!

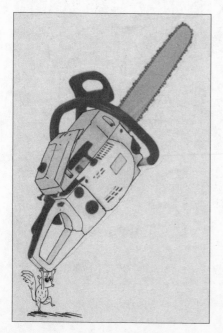

Note: At the time of writing this book, neither of these characters has found a home in any of our books as they are both currently serving 300-year prison sentences.

289

TRY THIS

Create a superhero or super-villain

Pick an ordinary object from the list below. Now imagine that it is the main weapon of a superhero. What would it be good for? How might it be used—for self-defence, attack, propulsion? Now start creating the character who uses this item—for example, Egg-beater Man ... he fights bad eggs.

Objects you could base your superhero or super-villain on:

- Rubber duck
- Tin opener
- Electric leaf blower
- Hairdryer
- Tweezers

- Toilet paper
- Fork
- Barbecue tongs
- Hammer
- Hamburger

40. That's embarrassing!

Everyone has been embarrassed at some time in their lives and these embarrassing memories can be a great source of story ideas. Though nobody likes being embarrassed, it can be very entertaining to watch someone else struggling with an embarrassing situation, especially if it's fictional.

In the Just stories, I enjoy putting Andy in as many embarrassing situations as possible. These include:

- Being chased down the street by the police while carrying his mother's handbag.

  'Andy's handbag', *Just Doomed!*

- Doing a stupid dive in front of the whole school, hitting his head on the bottom of the pool, knocking himself out and having to be rescued by Jeremy Smart, who he was actually trying to embarrass in the first place.

  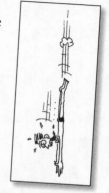

  'I hate Jeremy Smart!', *Just Doomed!*

- Celebrating his short-story competition win in front of the whole school when he hasn't actually won—Tanya Shepherd won with her story 'The Ballerina Princess'.

  'Kittens, puppies and ponies', *Just Crazy!*

- Sneezing chewed-up marshmallows all over the girl he has a crush on.

'Chubby bubbies', *Just Stupid!*

- Being naked or nearly naked in public ('Cockroach', 'Copycat from Ballarat', 'Runaway Pram,' 'In the Shower with Andy', 'Mudmen').

'Runaway pram, *Just Stupid!*

- Being the only clothed person in a nudist colony.

'Just nude!', *Just Doomed!*

The idea for *The Day My Bum Went Psycho* came from the fact that bums can be extremely embarrassing. They can release gas when you least expect them to. They can make noise when you least want them to. It's as if they have minds of their own. I just thought: what if bums really *did* have minds of their own and could detach themselves from our bodies and run away? Imagine how much more embarrassing that would be?!

Zack Freeman woke out of a deep sleep to see his bum perched on the ledge of his bedroom window. It was standing on two pudgy little legs, silhouetted against the moon, its little stick-like arms outstretched in front of it, as if it was about to dive.

Zack sat up in bed.

'No!' he yelled. 'Come back!'

But it was too late. His bum jumped out of the window and landed with a soft thud in the garden bed below.

Zack stared at the window and sighed.

'Oh no,' he said. 'Not again.'

This was not the first time Zack's bum had run away.

Since his twelfth birthday, two months ago, Zack's bum had made a habit of jumping off his body and running around the streets making a nuisance of itself. Zack was sick of it. So was the local bumcatcher who had already caught and impounded it three times.

Until recently Zack's bum had confined itself to a variety of harmless pranks, such as attaching itself to the faces of statues and passers-by.

But on its last outing it had joined a pack of five hundred feral bums who had lined the emergency stopping lane of the South Eastern Freeway and mooned all the people driving to work.

This stunt had caused many accidents, which the bums thought was a great laugh.

The sentencing judge, however, was not amused and placed them all on twelve-month good behaviour bonds.

The Day My Bum Went Psycho

TRY THIS

Embarrassing situations

Consider the following list of embarrassing situations and see if you can put them in order from least embarrassing to most embarrassing.

- Your fly is open (if you are a boy)
- You walk in on someone in the bathroom
- You are in public without your clothes on
- You break wind in public
- You are told off by your parent in front of your friends
- Your dress is caught up in your underpants (if you are a girl)
- You don't know what to say in a conversation
- You spill food or drink on somebody else
- You make up an excuse about why you can't go somewhere and then are caught out in the lie by the person you lied to
- You fall over in public
- You slip and fall over again when attempting to get up after falling over in public
- Your parents are kissing in front of you

... OR THIS

Illustrated list

Think about times you've been embarrassed. (If you're having trouble remembering an embarrassing moment, use the list of embarrassing situations from page 297 to help jog your memory.)

Make an illustrated list of five times that you've been embarrassed similar to the one on pages 292–293 of this chapter.

Things you could do with your illustrated list:

- Use it as the basis for a pocket book (see Chapter 31, page 223 for information on pocket books)

- Use it as the basis for a much longer list (e.g. 101 embarrassing situations)

- Choose one of the items on your list and use it as the basis for a comic strip or extended story (see Stretching the truth, page 275)

- If you are doing this as a class activity you could put them all together and make a book called *Embarrassing Stuff Our Class Has Done* ... or something like that. Put it in your library and share your embarrassment with the rest of the school.

ANDY GRIFFITHS

THE DAY MY BUM WENT PSYCHO

THE INTERNATIONAL BESTSELLER

BASED ON A TRUE STORY

41. The day my BLANK went BLANK!

I've always been excited by comics and movies with dramatic titles like *The Creature from the Black Lagoon*, *The Day the Earth Stood Still* and *The Night of the Living Dead*. I guess it's no surprise that I love making up my own over-the-top titles, although mine usually feature things that you don't generally think of as dangerous, e.g. pencils, koalas, grannies and bums.

I really like writing stories in which an ordinary everyday item—like a pencil—becomes scary and dangerous.

I didn't think there could possibly be a more stupid title for a book than *The Day My Bum Went Psycho*, but as I came to the end of the story and the Great White Bum was blasted out into space, the title *Zombie Bums from Uranus* came into my head and the whole thinking, wondering and story-making process started over again. In fact, it didn't stop until I'd written *Bumageddon: The final pongflict*.

Two of my favourite stupid, over-the-top titles.

KILLER MECHANICAL CHICKENS??

In the story 'Kittens, puppies and ponies' in *Just Crazy!*, Danny comes runner-up in the school short-story writing competition with his entry 'Killer Mechanical Chickens from Outer Space'. Flushed with confidence due to his story-writing success he now feels more than qualified to give Lisa some advice on storytelling.

'Well,' says Danny, sitting up in his chair and folding his arms. 'It's not that hard. You just need some sort of monster. It's not that important what it is. It can be an alien . . . or a robot . . . or even a chicken. It doesn't matter. It just has to be evil and want to destroy everything.'

Just Crazy!

I couldn't have said it better myself ... (Hang, on I *did* say it. Danny's just a character I created.)

The Very Bad Book

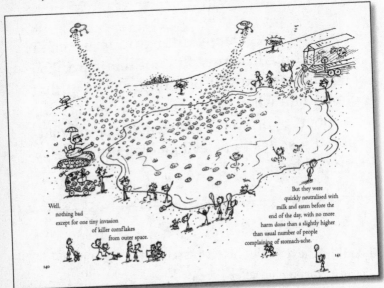

An invasion of killer cornflakes from outer space in 'The day nothing bad happened' (*The Bad Book*).

TRY THIS

Fill in the blanks

A good title is worth its weight in gold—both for getting the reader's attention and, hopefully, inspiring you to write a story to match. Try writing your own attention-grabbing title, a title that stops the reader in their tracks.

Some formulas you could use:

- Night of the Blanking Blanks!
- Invasion of the Blanky Blanks!
- Blood-sucking Blanks from the Blank!
- The Day my Blank went Blank!
- Giant Mutant Killer Blanks!
- Zombie Blanks from Blank!
- Killer Blanks from Blank!
- Blank-blanking, blank-blanking blanks!

NOW DO THIS

Design a book jacket

Select your favourite title from the previous exercise and design a book jacket for it. Think about an image that complements your title. And don't forget the blurb on the back cover. Remember, your blurb should give the reader a bit of an idea of what your story is about and should make it sound exciting and interesting—so readers immediately want to read it.

The 39-Storey Treehouse

42. To whom it may concern

Once when I was on holidays when I was little, I sent my grandmother a postcard that said DEAR GRANDMA, WE WENT SHOPPING AND I GOT COCOPOPS. This became a running joke in our family for many years, and when on holidays we would always send postcards telling each other nothing about the holiday except what we had for breakfast. Another part of the joke was to always choose the very worst postcard you could find. And an endless series of PSs and PPSs was pretty much compulsory.

I guess it's no surprise then that one of my best-known stories has featured a thinly disguised version of my favourite breakfast cereal and an endless series of PSs (25 in fact).

Why I love Choco-pops in fifty words or less

I love Choco-pops in fifty words or less because they are chocolaty, crunchy, cool, great, wonderful, amazing, exciting, lovely, yummy, etcetera.
Yours truly,
Andy Griffiths

P.S. That's exactly fifty words, even counting the 'Yours truly, Andy Griffiths'.

P.P.S. I could have given you many other reasons why I love Choco-pops, but I was only allowed fifty words.

P.P.P.S. If you'd let me have more words I would have told you about how I love Choco-pops so much that I once ate five bowls of them, one after the other.

I would have eaten a sixth bowl, too, except that I felt a bit sick and then, guess what? I really WAS sick! All over the kitchen floor. A big brown puddle of Choco-pops. Mum and Dad were really mad. Sooty was happy, though, because he dived in and started to eat them. Which just goes to show how great Choco-pops are— even dogs love them! In fact, Sooty probably likes them even more than I do, because as much as I love them I wouldn't eat Choco-pops that somebody else had already eaten and then thrown up. Not even if you paid me a million dollars.

P.P.P.P.S. Not even a trillion dollars.

P.P.P.P.P.S. Not even a million trillion dollars.

P.P.P.P.P.P.S. Well, MAYBE for a million trillion dollars. I'm not stupid, you know.

P.P.P.P.P.P.P.S. Please don't tell anybody about me eating the five bowls of Choco-pops and throwing up, because it would be kind of embarrassing if that got around, plus I told Mum and Dad that I'd only eaten three bowls and they would be really mad if they found out it was five. They are always going on about how Choco-pops are not very healthy and how they are full of sugar and blah blah blah blah, but parents are always saying stuff like that.

Just Shocking!

In the story 'Wish you weren't here' (from *Just Annoying!*), Andy borrows one of his neighbour's garden gnomes to take on holiday with him so that he can photograph the gnome having a good time and then send his neighbour the photograph as if it were a postcard from the gnome.

Dear Mrs Scott
Having a great tims.
Wish you were here.

    Love Your Garden Gnome
P.S. I had Cocoa Pops for breakfast!

Mrs Scott

12 Pleasant Drive

NICEVILLE

                          3756

Unfortunately, Andy's scheme doesn't go quite according to plan as he starts to imagine that the gnome is trying to kill him ... but that's another story.

You don't only have to send postcards from real places. You can send them from imaginary places too!

Another form of correspondence that I've always enjoyed is writing letters in the form of comic strips.

Here's an example of one I wrote from New Zealand.

WE SAW QUITE A LOT OF
SEALS — SOME WERE
ALIVE AND SOME WERE,
WELL, NOT-SO-ALIVE.

JILL & SARAH SAW A
SPERM WHALE BUT ALL
I SAW WAS THE INSIDE
OF A PLASTIC BUCKET.

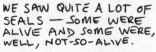
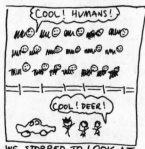

WE STOPPED TO LOOK AT
A FIELD OF DEER AND
EVERY SINGLE DEER
STOPPED TO LOOK AT US.

SARAH FED A **VERY**
HUNGRY LAMB

WE MET AN INJURED
PENGUIN CALLED LEWEY

AND WE GOT SQUEAKED
AT BY TWO WEIRD
GREEN BIRDS
♡ Andy

311

TRY THIS

Comic-strip letter

Write a letter in the form of a comic strip to an imaginary pen pal in another country describing:

- A typical day at school
- A recent holiday
- A school excursion
- A school camp
- A sporting event

... OR THIS

Imaginary postcard

Design a postcard for an imaginary destination. On the back of your picture write a short message to your family or best friend as if you were there (don't forget to tell them what you had for breakfast!).

Godzilla

baby

my hand

43. Toy stories

I have a large collection of weird and wonderful toys
collected from garage sales and op shops. Many of
my early attempts at writing stories began with me
photographing my toys having adventures out in the real
world, assembling the photographs and then writing brief
captions underneath. Then, as now, I loved trying to work
out what the reader might be expecting to happen and
then surprising them with something that they weren't
expecting.

For example, if a baby
and Godzilla met we
would probably expect
Godzilla to eat the baby.

What we wouldn't expect is for the baby to attempt to eat
Godzilla.

Another surprising thing that could happen would be for Godzilla to adopt the baby ...

or, even more surprising, for the baby to adopt Godzilla!

Or, perhaps most surprising of all,
for them to become friends,
fall in love ...

get married ...

and have children,
half Godzilla–half human …

or half human–
half Godzilla!

Getting into the habit of asking, 'How can I surprise my reader?' will not only help you to keep your reader entertained but will also help you to come up with many more potential storylines, ideas and characters.

Note: There's a video of Godzilla and the baby on YouTube at http://andygriffiths.com.au/links

TRY THIS

Reversals

One of the most reliable ways to surprise a reader is to use the technique of reversal. For instance, if you have a teacher and a student, we would normally expect the teacher to be in charge and the student to do what he or she is told. We would not expect the student to be in charge and the teacher to have to do what the student tells them to. This reversal of the normal order opens up all sorts of surprising story possibilities.

Try reversing each of the following scenarios. (I've made it easy for you ... all you have to do is to change the order of the words!)

Instead of a parent telling a child what to do,

the _____ tells their _____ what to do.

Instead of a person taking their dog for a walk,

the _____ takes their _____ for a walk.

Instead of a kid trying to squash a spider, a

_____ tries to squash a _____.

Draw a snapshot picture of each scene with speech bubble captions for each character so that we can hear as well as see them in their surprising new relationship (see Chapter 37 Snapshots, page 266).

44. Wasting the reader's time

You don't have to be a genius to know that being silly can be a lot of fun (which is how come I figured it out years ago). Telling stories provides plenty of opportunities for silliness and nonsense. Another way of thinking about nonsense is as a way of 'wasting the reader's time'. The surprising thing I've found is that many readers *love* having their time wasted!

For instance, we assume that when a story starts out it is going to make sense and that it will have a beginning, middle and end ... but it doesn't necessarily have to. In 'Barky the barking dog', the 'story' gets stuck on the one action ...

The 13-Storey Treehouse

Or, in the case of 'The very very very bad story' it gets stuck on the same two words for 11 pages until the book finally ends.

In fact things were SO bad that it made all the previous bad days seem like the good old days and the memory of those good old bad days made everybody cry and feel very sorry for themselves and feel even badder than they already did.

But eventually people started saying, 'Hey, we can't just sit around crying all day and feeling bad. We should try to fix things and make everything good again.'

So everybody got up, wiped their tears away, stopped feeling sorry for themselves and tried to make things good again.

But it was no use. The more they tried to make things good again, the badder things got. Things just got badder and

badder and badder.

THE END

The last page of *The Bad Book*.

But hey, if you think *I'm* good at wasting the reader's time, then you've obviously never done one of Terry's annoying page-number quests.

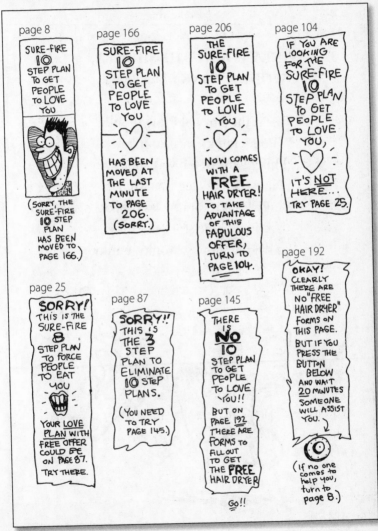

Just Doomed!

Sometimes a story might pretend to be telling you something when in fact it's not telling you anything that you don't already know from reading the title.

PINKY PONKY THE SHONKY, WONKY, BONKY DONKEY

This is the story of Pinky Ponky.
Pinky Ponky was a donkey.
Pinky Ponky's tail was shonky.
Pinky Ponky's leg was wonky.
Pinky Ponky's brain was bonky.
And that's the story of Pinky
Ponky: the shonky, wonky, bonky
donkey.

The Cat on the Mat is Flat

The adventures of melting teddy

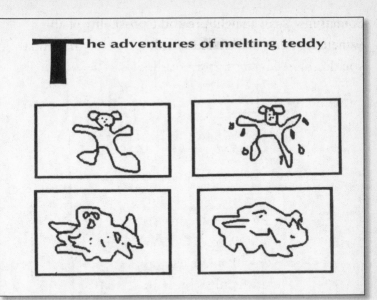

Mr Brainfright falls to pieces

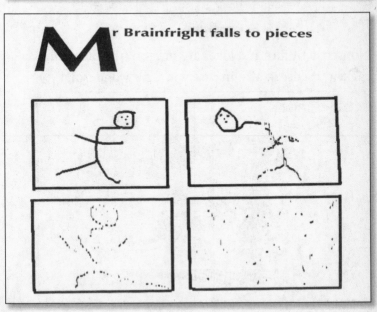

A nonsense story may hold out the possibility of an explanation that never comes.

The Dog That Fell Apart

Once upon a time there was a dog.

One day the dog's tail fell off.

The next day his legs fell off.

The next day his nose fell off.

The next day his ears fell off.

The next day his head fell off.

The next day was Tuesday.

THE END

The Very Bad Book

Nonsense riddles and jokes are fun too (the punchlines make no sense at all—in case you were wondering!).

Very Bad Riddles

Q: Why did the boy fall off his bike?

A: Because his mother threw a fridge at him.

The Bad Book

Two penguins were standing on an iceberg. One turned to the other and said, 'Radio.'

The Very Bad Book

TRY THIS

Write your own 'time-wasting' cartoon

Create your own 'time-wasting' cartoon in the style of 'Barky the barking dog'. There are many possible characters you could have fun with.

For example:

- Buzzy the buzzing fly
- Purry the purring cat
- Mooey the mooing cow
- Chirpy the chirping bird
- Hooty the hooting owl
- Roary the roaring lion
- Pooey the pooing parrot
- Fighty the fighting fish
- Argy Bargy the angry aardvark
- Beeep the foul-mouthed kitten
- Snoozy the slowest snail in the world

... OR THIS

Rubber-stamp story

And hey, you can waste a lot of time creating stupid stories with a rubber stamp, or even better a whole set.

STAMPEDE: AN AFRICAN ADVENTURE

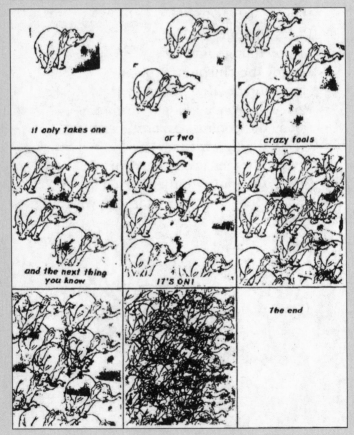

it only takes one

or two

crazy fools

and the next thing you know

IT'S ON!

The end

45. What if ... ?

I'm not completely sure where ideas come from but I've learned that one of the fastest and most reliable ways of generating lots of them is to get into the habit of asking 'what if?' as often as possible. This simple question is a surefire generator of story scenarios. A lot of my stories— especially those in the Just series—are developed by asking a series of what-if questions, as the following examples show.

'Are we there yet?' (*Just Annoying!*)

WHAT IF your parents threatened to stop the car and make you get out and walk home if you didn't stop being annoying, and **WHAT IF** you didn't stop being annoying and they really did stop the car and made you get out in the middle of nowhere and then drove away? And then **WHAT IF** a bikie picked you up and rode after your parents to try to catch up with them but they didn't stop because they thought they were being chased by a mad bikie and then **WHAT IF** you tried to jump from the speeding bike onto your parents' car?

What if your parents made you get out
of the car and then drove away?

'Mudmen' (*Just Crazy!*)

WHAT IF you got locked out of the house with your dad and you were both in the nude? And then **WHAT IF** you both covered yourselves in mud and ran through the neighbourhood to get to your dad's office to retrieve the spare house key? And then **WHAT IF** it started to rain and all the mud washed off? And then **WHAT IF** your dad's boss and his wife saw you?

What if you got locked out of the house and you were naked?

'Just nude!' (*Just Doomed!*)

WHAT IF for your next family holiday your dad accidentally booked you all into a nudist resort? And then **WHAT IF** your family all decided to stay and started taking their clothes off right in the reception area? And then **WHAT IF** you ran out of reception with your clothes on and were chased by a whole lot of angry nude people?

What if your dad accidentally booked
a family holiday at a nudist resort?

Terry imagines a WHAT IF scenario in *The 13-Storey Treehouse*.

TRY THIS

Create your own WHAT IF story outline

Fill in the blanks of the following WHAT IF outline. You can use one of the 'What if?' scenarios below or come up with one of your own. Maybe you'll get a scenario or an idea that you can use as the basis for a story or cartoon like the one on the previous page. Or maybe you'll just have a bit of fun. Either way you'll get invaluable practice with the what-iffing technique.

- What if you discovered that your parents were zombies?
- What if storms could come inside and into your bedroom?
- What if you woke up and found yourself transformed into a giant stick insect?
- What if you accidentally un-invented gravity in your science class?

WHAT IF _____

and then **WHAT IF** _____

and then **WHAT IF** _____

_____ ?

Resources

Random idea generator

One of my favourite ways to generate a
character and/or story idea is to make a list of
adjectives on one side of the page and a list of
nouns on the other. Then I mix and match
until I find a character or idea that inspires
me to start writing.

A fun way to work with the lists is to write out the
numbers 1 to 26 and all the letters of the alphabet and then
cut them all up (make sure you keep your numbers and
letters separate).

You should now have a pile of numbers and a pile of
letters. Select a number from your number pile and a letter
from your letter pile. Match these with the corresponding
words in List 1 and List 2. (For example, if you had the
number 20 and the letter T your random title would be 'The
evil Barbie doll'.) If you like the combination, use it as the
starting point for a story. If not, try again. (You can also add
the settings list when doing this activity.)

Note: If you are a teacher doing this with a class, you can write
each of the words on a separate card and then hand each student
an adjective card and a noun card (and a setting) and challenge
them to write about their combination. You are, of course, free
to make up your own random lists. Mine are simply intended to
provide a starting point.

LIST 1: Adjective

1. jealous
2. shy
3. boastful
4. rude
5. bad-tempered
6. dancing
7. ugly
8. melting
9. exploding
10. smelly
11. crazy
12. stupid
13. flying
14. disgusting
15. electric
16. mysterious
17. nude
18. magic
19. swearing
20. evil
21. bouncing
22. lazy
23. killer
24. mutant
25. clever
26. annoying

LIST 2: Noun

A. pencil
B. baby
C. dinosaur
D. old man
E. television
F. dog
G. clown
H. teacher
I. brother
J. sister
K. teddy
L. spider
M. kangaroo
N. garbage truck
O. book
P. toilet
Q. monster
R. banana
S. cake
T. Barbie doll
U. computer
V. underpants
W. penguin
X. cow
Y. robot
Z. granny

LIST 3: Setting

i. supermarket
ii. office
iii. school
iv. spaceship
v. treehouse
vi. car wash
vii. train
viii. plane
ix. farm
x. zoo
xi. disco
xii. dentist
xiii. circus
xiv. desert
xv. library
xvi. police station
xvii. hospital
xviii. museum
ixx. church
xx. swimming pool
xxi. garden
xxii. forest
xxiii. ship
xxiv. cinema
xxv. bath
xxvi. restaurant

A guide to Andy and Terry's books

The JUST series

A popular series of funny, fast-paced short stories told by young Andy, who considers himself the world's greatest, craziest and most annoying practical joker.

Just Tricking!, *Just Annoying!*, *Just Stupid!*, *Just Crazy!*, *Just Disgusting!*, *Just Shocking!*, *Just Doomed!* and *Just Macbeth!* (a script based on Shakespeare's *Macbeth*, featuring the characters from the Just series).

The BAD books

Packed with crazy cartoons, revolting rhymes, putrid poems, dumb drawings, bad riddles, bad jokes, cautionary tales and bad characters doing bad things, the Bad Books will catapult you into a topsy-turvy world in which everything good is bad and everything bad is VERY bad!

The Bad Book, *The Very Bad Book* and *Killer Koalas from Outer Space* (an anthology of some of the least worst bits of the two Bad Books).

The FLAT CAT and BIG FAT COW series

A joyously silly series propelled by kid-pleasing, tongue-tripping verse and edgy, stick-figure-filled illustrations. Ideal for beginning or reluctant readers, but will delight readers of all ages and abilities.

The Cat on the Mat is Flat,
The Big Fat Cow That Goes Kapow

The TREEHOUSE books

Illustrated novels featuring Andy and Terry, a writer and illustrator who live in an amazing, ever-expanding treehouse. Ridiculously silly adventures crammed with ridiculously silly pictures.

The 13-Storey Treehouse, The 26-Storey Treehouse

The SCHOOLING AROUND series

A set of four novels chronicling the amazing goings on at Northwest Southeast Central School. Sure to appeal to both confident and emerging readers of all ages, they are also ideal for both parents and classroom teachers to read aloud.

Treasure Fever!, Pencil of Doom!, Mascot Madness!, Robot Riot!

The BUM trilogy

The epic Bum trilogy tells the story of Zack Freeman, his crazy runaway bum, a crack bum-fighting unit called the B-team and some of the biggest, ugliest and meanest bums ever to roam the face of the Earth.

The Day My Bum Went Psycho, Zombie Bums from Uranus, Bumageddon: The Final Pongflict

Andy & Terry's WONDERFUL WORLD OF STUPIDITY

Andy & Terry's Wonderful World of Stupidity is a series of seriously silly, fully illustrated 100% fact-free guide books that aim to present as much unscientific data and misinformation as it's possible to cram into a series of seriously silly, fully illustrated 100% fact-free guide books.

What Bumosaur is That?, What Body Part is That?

Andypedia

The Andypedia is a complete guide to every book, every story and every character in the world of Andy Griffiths' books. Available as an ebook only.

http://momentumbooks.com.au/books/andypedia/

The Naked Boy and the Crocodile (edited by Andy Griffiths)

A collection of stories written by children from remote Indigenous communities in Australia. Written in simple picture-book formats (pocket books), these tales are surprising, funny and touching ... and sometimes true! All proceeds from the book are donated to the Indigenous Literacy Foundation (www.indigenousliteracyfoundation.org.au).

Once upon a Slime: 45 Fun Ways to Get Writing ... *Fast*!

Designed for teachers, students and young aspiring writers, *Once upon a Slime* contains 45 fun writing activities, such as lists, instructions, cartoons, personal stories, poems and pocket books.

Examples from Andy and Terry's books are used throughout to demonstrate techniques and to inspire readers to have as much fun playing with ideas, words and pictures as Andy and Terry do when they get together to create their crazy books.

More information at http://www.andygriffiths.com.au

Index of writing forms/ types of activities

Acknowledgements

Yes, that's right: I've written another list.

This one is a list of all the people who have helped me over the years and to whom I'd like to say a big thank you:

1. My grandma for her constant encouragement and for keeping that spooky old copy of *Struwwelpeter* that both terrified and amused me in equal measure and has provided such a reliable compass for my own writing.

2. My parents for everything, really, but especially for filling our bookshelves with all the other essentials (apart from *Struwwelpeter*): Coles Funny Picture Books, Lewis Carroll, The Complete Brothers Grimm, Dr Seuss and Enid Blyton, as well as for supplying me with pens, pencils, paper, time and then getting out of my way and leaving me to get on with it.

3. My sisters Susan and Julie for still being nice to me despite the fact that their memories of our childhood suggest that I was probably a lot more like the extremely annoying character Andy from the Just series than I remember or would care to admit.

4. My best friend Danny Pickett and primary-school crush Lisa Mackney for being incredibly good sports about me borrowing their names for their fictional

345

counterparts in the Just series. Especially Danny since he's been portrayed as far more stupid than he is in real life and, in fact, as far more stupid than any human could possibly be. He is definitely not stupid and has grown up to be an extremely talented landscape gardener. Lisa, on the other hand, is every bit as beautiful as described in the books and works as a relief teacher in the eastern suburbs of Melbourne. If you see her, please tell her I said hi.

5. My crazy dog Sooty whose twelve-year mission to chase and bite the tyres of speeding cars taught me the importance of having clear goals, total commitment, patience, persistence and healthy teeth.

6. My neighbour Mrs Broadbent for giving me a thesaurus for my 12th birthday when I didn't even know what a thesaurus was.

7. Mrs Woolmer, my high school librarian, who stocked our library with wonderfully unsuitable and unsavoury titles like *13 Ways to Dispose of a Body*, which helped build a bridge from my beloved horror comics into the world of adult fiction.

8. My year 11 English teacher Mr Bechervaise for not only bringing a sense of humour to the English classroom but for being an active model of creativity by writing poems, taking photographs, making films, directing

plays and editing the school magazine. He also introduced me to *The Catcher in the Rye* for which I will be forever in his debt.

9. All the members of my various bands including *Silver Cylinder*, *The Unborn Babies*, *Gothic Farmyard*, *The Horns of Doom* and *Skippy the Butcher* for letting me write the lyrics and shout them into the microphone despite my obvious lack of any sort of musical aptitude whatsoever.

10. Staff and students at Mildura High School 1989–90 and especially the members of our teacher writing group: Andy Edwards, Judi Harris, Andrew 'Mad Dog' Morgan, Kim Patterson, Robyn Paull, Mark Storm and Hilary Thiele.

11. Inspirational writing teachers Barry Dickins and Carmel Bird, who both appeared when I needed them most, as well as humour and public speaking coach Pete Crofts. And even though I've never studied with her in person, I'd like to thank Natalie Goldberg for writing the best book about writing ever written— *Writing Down the Bones*.

12. Longman Cheshire publisher Rina Leeuwenberg for taking a chance on *Swinging on the Clothesline* and for having the brilliant idea to get Terry Denton to illustrate it.

13. Terry Denton for agreeing to illustrate *Swinging on the Clothesline* (and almost everything else I've written since), and for being such a fantastic artist, co-writer, clown, friend and general all-round genius who, when you ask him a question like, 'What should we put on the cover of *Just Doomed!*?' answers, 'How about a horse in a blender?' Well, of course!

14. Early supporters Agnes Nieuwenhuizen, Mike Shuttleworth, Jenny Stubbs, Lynne Ellis and Lauris Pandolfini and her Booked Out Speakers Agency, who helped me keep my head above water in the early years by spreading the word to schools and helping me to generate a living as a visiting author. Thanks also to all the organisers of Australia's Children's Choice Awards: YABBA (Vic), KOALA (NSW), COOL (ACT), KROC (NT), BILBY (QLD), WAYBRA (WA) and to all the students who vote for their favourite books each year.

15. Reed-for-Kids Publisher Janet Rowe for being able to see the potential in the 200 practical jokes that formed the first draft of *Just Tricking!* and providing the valuable guidance that helped me to completely rewrite it.

16. Publisher Jean Feiwel, without whose enthusiasm my runaway butts, flat cats, exploding cows and killer koalas would never have had the chance to invade the USA.

17. Literary agents Debbie Golvan, Fiona Inglis and Jill Grinberg who I'd not only *like* to thank for all their hard work but whom I'm *contractually obliged* to thank as they are entitled to a percentage of all my published writing, including my acknowledgements.

18. The fantastic team at Pan Macmillan who have been my publishers since 1997. I have been lucky to work closely with many wonderful people over the years, including publisher Anna McFarlane, sales co-ordinators Phil Lawson and Katie Crawford, editor Catherine Day and publicists Jane Novak, Anyez Lindop, Sue Bobbermein and Jane Symmans. Very special thanks to publishing director Cate Paterson for bringing me on board and for her continuing support, advice, encouragement and friendship. Thanks also to my endlessly creative and apparently indefatigable publisher Claire Craig (without whose gentle—and not so gentle—persistence *Once upon a Slime* and many other books would no doubt still be on the drawing board), freelance copy-editor Ali Lavau and in-house editor Samantha Sainsbury (for making me look like a much better writer than I actually am), designer Liz Seymour (who has designed and set every single book!) and last, but not least, senior publicist Kate Nash without whose boundless energy and good humour book promotion and book tours would be nowhere near as much fun.

19. The Indigenous Literacy Foundation—especially Karen Williams, Kristin Gill, Suzy Wilson, David Gaunt and Deb Danks for being such great travelling companions and for giving me the opportunity to meet and work with so many wonderful students and teachers in remote Indigenous communities. (Visit www.indigenousliteracyfoundation.org.au to find out how you can help to level the playing field for all Australian students no matter what part of Australia they live in.)

20. The Bell Shakespeare company, in particular Gill Perkins, Marion Potts and Wayne Harrison, whose support and expertise helped Jill and I to turn one of Shakespeare's most terrifying plays into a fun night out for the whole family.

21. Markus Zusak for being such a generous friend— always happy to share his insights, inspirations and musical discoveries via a constant stream of books and compilation CDs.

22. My daughter Jasmine whose willingness to believe practically anything I told her as a young child helped me take my storytelling ability to a whole new level.

23. My other daughter Sarah for her enthusiasm, helpful ideas and editing suggestions, and without whom the covers of the bum trilogy would not have been anywhere near as memorable (nor as controversial).

24. Jill Griffiths my editor, collaborator, wife and best friend, with whom I work closely in the creation of every book right from the earliest drafts through to the final pages, the final final pages, the final final final pages and all the final pages beyond that.

25. The wonderful booksellers of Australia and, of course, all of my readers, including the many passionate children, parents and teachers who have attended events, bought my books, laughed at my jokes and written so many beautiful letters of support, encouragement and gratitude over the years—I am honoured and touched and deeply grateful.

26. You, for reading right to the end—unless you just skipped straight to this last item, in which case thanks for nothing because I put a lot of work into this stupid list and the least you could have done is read the whole thing!

NO! It's the end of the book!!

**The Day My Bum Went Psycho,
Foiled an Invasion of Zombie Bums
from Uranus and Saved the World from
Complete and Utter Bumageddon!**

All three books in the epic BUM saga condensed and
fully illarsetrated in one stench-packed volume.

Zack sat up in bed.
'No!' he yelled. 'Come back!'
But it was too late. His bum jumped out the window and
    landed with a soft thud in the garden below.
'Oh no,' he sighed. 'Not again.'

COMING APRIL 2014

DIGITAL ANDY

**It's an encyclopedia ...
all about Andy!**

The *Andypedia* is a complete guide to every book, every story and every character in the world of Andy Griffiths' books. It's also a complete guide to everything you ever wanted to know about Andy himself—including the answers to questions people are always asking him, like 'How old were you when you started writing?' and 'How many books have you actually written?' and 'Where do you get your ideas from?' and 'Did all that stuff *really* happen to you?' and 'Was Danny Pickett *really* your best friend?' and 'Were you *really* in love with Lisa Mackney?' and 'Did your bum *really* grow arms and legs and run away?'

Available exclusively in digital
from all good ebook retailers.